SCHILLER AND MUSIC

UNIVERSITY OF NORTH CAROLINA
STUDIES IN THE GERMANIC LANGUAGES
AND LITERATURES

For other volumes in this series see page 202.

NUMBER FIFTY-FOUR

UNIVERSITY
OF NORTH CAROLINA
STUDIES IN
THE GERMANIC LANGUAGES
AND LITERATURES

Schiller and Music

by R. M. LONGYEAR

Associate Professor of Music, University of Kentucky

CHAPEL HILL
THE UNIVERSITY OF NORTH CAROLINA PRESS

Printed in the Netherlands by Royal VanGorcum Ltd., Assen

To Katie

TABLE OF CONTENTS

Friedrich Schiller's career spanned two of the major epochs in German cultural history: the *Sturm und Drang* and Weimar Classicism. His many activities – dramatist, poet, philosopher, literary and social critic, historian, physician, and educator – are truly astounding in their diversity. A study of his life reveals the importance which music played in it; an investigation of his literary work shows the significance of music in heightening dramatic action, as characterizing agent, or as metaphor; a reading of his philosophical writings discloses that music played an ancillary but not negligible role in his aesthetic system. Schiller influenced the music of his time and afterwards not only because his poems became texts for vocal music or his dramas became opera librettos or subjects for program music, but also because of his ideas on the moral nature and seriousness of art.

Such recent writers as Jürgen Mainka and Wolfgang Seifert have strongly expressed their dissatisfaction with the existing literature concerning Schiller's relationship to music, for virtually all of it consists of occasional studies, mostly for anniversaries of his birth or death, which are either discussions of a limited aspect of his interest in music or are vague, broad surveys for the general reader. The few exceptions – Brandstaeter's pioneering study (1863), the essays in the Schiller issue of *Die Musik* (1905), and Knudsen's doctoral dissertation (1908) – are brief and are outmoded because of the information both about Schiller and about the music of his time which has become available during the past six decades; furthermore, question-begging and bias characterize the attempts to connect Schiller's musical aesthetics with the music of his time, and relatively few of the compositions based on Schiller's works have been studied. For these reasons, a new investigation of the topic 'Schiller and Music' is necessary, if only to complement the many investigations of the relationship of Goethe and Herder to this art.

The procedure of this study has consisted of asking certain questions. Although they are not universally applicable, the student of the importance of music in a writer's life and work can ask them in the course of his investigations.

i. What role did music play in Schiller's life? What were his formative musical experiences? What was the musical competence of his friends? What music could he hear? To what extent did he participate in musical activities, either as a performer or a listener?

ii. What use, as a dramatist, did Schiller make of incidental music? What precedents and which of his predecessors influenced him? Who wrote his incidental music, how did Schiller like it, and under what conditions was it used?

iii. How did Schiller use music in dramatic characterization and poetic metaphor? Is there a 'musical' poetic language?

iv. To what extent did Schiller regard music in his aesthetic philosophy? Who influenced his ideas on music? How did he employ musical and aesthetic terminology to describe an art with which he was not technically conversant? How did he regard the various musical genres and the composers of his time, and are his formal aesthetic views on music and his opinions of specific works in any way related? Did his musical philosophy influence subsequent generations?

v. How did Schiller think his works should be set to music and how did he regard the attempts of his contemporaries to put music to his words? Which subsequent composers did he inspire and how did they use his dramatic and poetic works as texts for art-songs and cantatas, librettos for operas, or subjects for program music?

The principal sources for this study have been Schiller's dramas, poems, philosophical works, correspondence, and the compositions based on Schiller's writings. Since there are several different editions of letters to and from Schiller, I have indicated the date of the letter rather than the pages of the collection in which it is printed, for one can reasonably assume that all the letters will eventually be collected in the *Nationalausgabe* of Schiller's complete works. The ravages of World War II had the side effect of destroying most of the unpublished music to Schiller's works, and what little has survived has been preserved mostly by accident.

Space limitations do not permit me to acknowledge the contributions of all those who helped with this study, but I would like to give special thanks to Karl and Editha Neumann, Donald Grout, Eric Werner, Karl-Heinz Hahn, Robert Münster, Lee S. Greene, and particularly Lothar Hoffmann-

Erbrecht and Reinhard Buchwald, for their friendly
advice, assistance, and encouragement. I owe much
to the help of the reference divisions of the libraries
of Cornell University, the University of Southern
Mississippi, and the University of Tennessee, and
to the music divisions of the Library of Congress,
the University of North Carolina, and the Bayerische
Staatsbibliothek. The Goethe-Schiller Archiv in
Weimar, the Weimar Nationaltheater, the Bären-
reiter-Verlag in Kassel, and the Friedrich-Schiller-
Universität in Jena most kindly sent publications and
microfilms, mostly without cost, of material and
manuscripts unobtainable here. Much of the initial
research was aided through an appointment as a
Visiting Scholar at Cornell University during the
summer of 1962, and subsequent study was facili-
tated by the excellent Germanics collection at the
University of Tennessee and a grant from the
Kentucky Research Foundation. I owe special
thanks to Ramona Cormier for her suggestions
concerning Chapter IV and to Thomas B. Stroup for
his editorial advice. Nevertheless, the errors in this
study are mine and mine alone.

Finally, my biggest debt of gratitude, to my wife,
I can only partially repay by dedicating this study
to her.

Lexington, Kentucky   R. M. LONGYEAR

ABBREVIATIONS

DR   *Deutsche Rundschau*

Geiger   Ludwig Geiger, ed., *Briefwechsel zwischen Schiller und Körner*. Stuttgart and Berlin, 1892, 4 vols.

Grove   Eric Blom (ed.), *Grove's Dictionary of Music and Musicians*, 5th. ed. London, 1954

JAMS   *Journal of the American Musicological Society*

JMP   *Jahrbuch der Musikbibliothek Peters*

Jonas   Fritz Jonas, ed., *Schillers Briefe*. Stuttgart, 1892, 7 vols.

MGG   Friedrich Blume, ed., *Die Musik in Geschichte und Gegenwart*. Kassel, 1951

M & L   *Music and Letters*

MQ   *Musical Quarterly*

PMLA   *Publications of the Modern Language Association*

SA   *Schillers sämtliche Werke*, Säkular-Ausgabe. Leipzig, n.d., 16 vols.

SGTG   *Schriften der Gesellschaft für Theatergeschichte*

SP   Max Hecker and Julius Peterson, eds., *Schillers Persönlichkeit*. Weimar, 1904, 3 vols.

Sulzer   Johann Georg Sulzer, *Allgemeine Theorie der schönen Künste*, 2d. ed., Leipzig, 1792, 4 vols.

    K   articles by Kirnberger

    S   articles by Schulz

    K-S   articles by Kirnberger and Schulz

Suphan   Bernhard Suphan, ed., *Herders sämmtliche Werke*. Berlin, 1878, 33 vols.

That music permeated the life of Friedrich Schiller is shown not only in his writings and letters but also in the reminiscences of his contemporaries, and to realize the extent of his knowledge of music and its personal significance to him is to realize its value in his literary and philosophical works. We should look, therefore, first at music in his life.

Schiller was not born into a musical family. His father, a captain in the army of Karl Eugen, Duke of Württemberg, is not known to have had any inclination toward either music or literature. His mother, an innkeeper's daughter, liked the 'geistliche Lieder,' or spiritual songs, by Klopstock, Gellert, and Uz, and it is significant that those who discuss this aspect of Schiller's childhood mention the poets rather than the composers.[1] Young Fritz, whose childhood ambition was to be a Lutheran minister, was more influenced by the words than the tunes, which were simple melodies in a folklike style rather than the sturdy Lutheran chorales of the Reformation or the arrangements of them by J. S. Bach. The organ improvisations which he heard in the church at Ludwigsburg were probably a stronger musical influence than the spiritual songs, for he later referred to the organ as the creator of an atmosphere of solemnity in *Die Jungfrau von Orleans* and his essay, 'Über Anmut und Würde.'

Opera, however, was the principal musical diet of his childhood and youth. Between 1753 and 1769 Karl Eugen and his musical director, Niccolò Jommelli, created one of the most magnificent musical establishments of the century and strove to

obtain the finest singers, musicians, and dancers in
Europe to satisfy Karl Eugen's passion for music,
which Burney described as being 'as strong as that of
the emperor Nero.'[2] Jommelli's operas demanded immense resources: for example, *Vologese* required,
among other things, 24 councillors, 200 soldiers,
60 spectators, and 250 supers as 'spectators' in the
amphitheatre.

The objections of the citizens of Stuttgart to the
extravagance of Karl Eugen's opera caused him to
move his court to Ludwigsburg, while the opposition
of the Württembergers increased to the point of
formal complaints to the Imperial Diet. One aspect
of public resistance was the refusal of the citizens to
attend the opera; to counter this and to give the
appearance of a full house and thus impress visiting
dignitaries, Karl Eugen compelled his officers to
dress in civilian clothes and attend the operatic
performances, often with their families. Captain
Schiller was evidently not exempted from this
regulation, and thus both Fritz and his older sister
Christophine were taken to the opera.

Although Karl Eugen's love for music began to
cool in 1767 and Jommelli was released in 1769, the
opera in Ludwigsburg was still magnificent enough
to thrill the Schiller children. Christophine remi-
nisced in 1845 that even though the operas were
given in Italian, 'the decorations and the splendid
costumes were enough for us.' The nine-year-old
Fritz was impressed by the rapid changes of scenery,
the animals on the stage, the grand entries, the dances,
and the great singers accompanied by an excellent

orchestra.[3] The memories of the *opere serie* by Jommelli were to affect not only Schiller's ideas on opera but also most of his dramas.

Music played an important role at the Karlsschule, founded by Karl Eugen in 1770 and to which Captain Schiller was forced to send his son. The orchestra and the opera gave frequent programs, and since all of the students were either on the stage or in the audience, young Schiller heard many of the finest operas of the time. He acted in the prologue to Sacchini's *Callirroë*, the last major opera to be written for Karl Eugen, and in 1780 he took the title role in a production of Goethe's drama *Clavigo*, which contains some incidental music. Although some symphonies and overtures by Handel, Haydn, the Mannheim composers, and either C. P. E. or J. C. Bach may have been performed by the orchestra, which was occasionally rehearsed personally by the Duke, the musical repertoire at the Karlsschule was almost exclusively Italian. Agostino Poli, who succeeded Boroni as musical director in 1775, was hostile to German music and restricted the operatic productions to Italian works and *Singspiele* written by students, but the nucleus of the school's musical library consisted of Jommelli's operas.

Schiller's first surviving dramatic attempt, *Semele*, is in the style of a libretto for an *opera seria*. Written in 1779, it was first published as a 'lyrical operetta' in his *Anthologie für das Jahr 1782*. *Semele* is merely an attempt at opera, for there are no indications in the text for the placement of recitatives, arias, or ensembles; where music is specified, the designations

are indistinguishable from the requirements for
incidental music in the spoken drama. The demands
on the stage manager resemble the extravagances of
Baroque machine opera, and Schiller's friend
Streicher commented that *Semele* was such a gran-
diose conception that all of the mechanical arts of
the theatre would be insufficient for its staging.[4]
Thus during Schiller's lifetime *Semele* was never set
to music (although in 1900 an unsuccessful attempt
was made in Berlin to put music from Handel's
Semele to this drama), and the poet later repudiated
this work with the remark: 'The mention of *Semele*
ordinarily frightens me. May Apollo and his nine
muses forgive me for sinning so grievously against
them.'[5]

After his graduation from the Karlsschule Schiller
was extremely unhappy with his garrison duties as a
regimental surgeon, which were not onerous but
boring and poorly remunerated. He spent most of
his spare time in revising *Die Räuber*, begun during
his student days, and in writing the poems later to be
published in the *Anthologie für das Jahr 1782*, but he
found occasion to meet his musical friends from
among his classmates at the Karlsschule, especially
a convivial drinking companion named Johann
Rudolf Zumsteeg, the first composer to set his works
to music. Schiller's circle of musical acquaintances
was soon widened by two clavier players, Luise
Dorothea Vischer and Andreas Streicher.

Luise Vischer, the 'Laura' of the love poems in the
Anthologie, attracted Schiller although she was eight

years his senior and a widow with two children. Christophine described her as a thin blonde with watery blue eyes. The poem 'Laura am Klavier' has raised questions concerning Frau Vischer's musicality: Minna Körner remembered Schiller's describing her playing 'gut Klavier' and making an excellent glass of punch, whereas Scherrl stated that she was 'slightly musical.' [6]

Parzeller has stated that the music of Carl Philipp Emanuel Bach inspired 'Laura am Klavier,' [7] and it is most likely that Schiller became acquainted with this composer's music through his friendship with Andreas Streicher, who saw him at a public examination at the Karlsschule and was later introduced to him by Zumsteeg. Streicher and Schiller soon became close friends because of their many common interests; Streicher found that his views, especially on poetry and music, were 'completely new, unusual, convincing, and natural in the highest degree.' [8]

Their friendship was soon put to a strong test when Schiller decided to escape from Stuttgart. Karl Eugen had noticed him adversely even during his student days, [8a] and the events which arose from the first performance and publication of *Die Räuber* were climactic: he was summoned before the Duke, called 'Er,' and forbidden to publish anything but medical articles or to correspond with persons outside of Württemberg. Because he subsequently absented himself without leave to attend a performance of his drama in Mannheim, Karl Eugen placed him under house arrest.

Punished, disappointed, and bored, the poet decided to escape the stultifying atmosphere of Stuttgart; after confiding in Streicher, who promised his assistance, the two friends left Stuttgart on the night of 22 September 1782, with two trunks and a clavichord packed in the coach which took them to Mannheim. During his first stay in Mannheim he remained indoors, revising *Fiesko* after its rejection by the Nationaltheater, and hiding for fear of being kidnapped and returned as a military prisoner to Stuttgart. A welcome diversion from arduous labor, disappointment, and fear was provided by Streicher's clavichord playing, the effect of which on Schiller he later described as follows:

> Even in Stuttgart sad or lively music took him outside himself and appropriate clavier playing aroused all emotions in him. At the noon meal he would ask [me] to play for him that evening. At twilight [I] would play while Schiller walked up and down in a room frequently illuminated only by moonlight, and would break out into unintelligible, animated speech.[9]

While stranded in Worms by snow and cold Schiller, Streicher, and some friends attended a performance of Georg Benda's melodrama *Ariadne auf Naxos*. Although the quality of the performance was 'ridiculous,' Schiller was highly impressed with what to him was a novel form of dramatic music, watched the performance with 'earnest, deep gaze,' was 'completely lost in it as if he had never seen anything similar or would be seeing it for the last time,' and refused to join his friends in making fun of the performance.[10]

In 1783 the two friends were parted – Streicher to stay in Mannheim to study with one of the musicians who still remained after the glorious orchestra had been dissolved in 1778, Schiller to move to Bauerbach where he could work undisturbed either by financial worries or threats from Karl Eugen. In a parting letter Schiller gave his friend some valuable advice:

> You are young, far enough along in your art in order to be useful. Study under a master in a large city in which you know there is much activity, avoid becoming mechanical in your art, make yourself useful [to your teacher] and find first of all the opportunity to study the man, earn a living, and when you leave [get] a recommendation. The great Titian ground colors for Raphael. This was by no means a disgrace; it gave his name the greater honor.[11]

At the end of July 1783 Schiller returned to Mannheim to accept a contract offered by Count Dalberg, the Intendant of the theatre, for the production of *Fiesko* and *Kabale und Liebe*, but after the latter drama was produced his contract was not renewed. In May Schiller wrote Henriette von Wolzogen, his hostess at Bauerbach, that he had received four letters from Leipzig, one of which contained a setting of the song 'Schön wie Engel' from *Die Räuber*, 'something that

would be agreeable to me.' The letters were from
Ferdinand Huber; Dora Stock, who made a celebrated drawing of Mozart when he visited Dresden
in 1789; her sister Minna; and Minna's fiancé,
Christian Gottfried Körner, who was to exercise a
strong influence on the development of Schiller's
musical and aesthetic ideas.

Because his prospects for future advancement in
Mannheim were dim, Schiller left on 9 April 1785.
The cordial tone of the letters from his new friends
implied that he would be warmly welcomed and
influenced his decision to move to Saxony. He
announced his impending arrival with a discussion
of his drama in progress, *Don Carlos*, and how 'in
your circle I will play more happily and more
intimately on my lute.'[13]

He found his new friends in Leipzig, and subsequently Dresden, altogether delightful. Staying at
Körner's home was a pleasure, for Schiller noticed
that 'today on waking I heard the piano being played
above me; you cannot believe how it cheered me.'[14]
The concerts and social gatherings at which music
was informally performed also pleased him. The
Leipzig bookseller Göschen recalled how two
theology students would frequently make music and
that Schiller would participate, 'though probably
just as a listener.' Luise Pistorius met Schiller in
Dresden, where he invited her and her father, the
bookseller Schwan who had previously befriended
him in Mannheim, to a concert at which the Körners
sang, and Luise saw Schiller for the last time at a
concert in Körner's home.[15] The leading musical

personages to whom he was introduced were Johann Gottfried Naumann, the musical director in Dresden who wrote Italianate operas and is said to have composed the 'Dresden Amen,' and Johann Adam Hiller, the composer of many *Singspiele*.

Since life in Dresden was enjoyable (at least from a musical standpoint) but unremunerative, Schiller moved in July of 1787 to Weimar, a step which his brother-in-law Reinwald and Schwan had urged him to take as early as 1783. He was already known there through his earlier dramas, his novel *Der Geister-seher*, and subsequently his historical studies, which were to earn him a professorship at the University of Jena two years later; furthermore, he had read the first act of *Don Carlos* to the Duke, Karl August, on Christmas of 1784. The warm reception he received in Weimar during his first visit in July 1787 induced him to stay; here and at Jena he was to spend the rest of his life, except for occasional excursions.

Weimar was the seat of letters and philosophy in Germany during the last quarter of the eighteenth century, much as the Vienna of Haydn, Mozart, and Beethoven was the city for music. Not even London or Paris could boast such a constellation of geniuses as Schiller, Goethe, Herder, and Wieland. The concept of general intellectual culture held by these men affected not only Germany but also the world: the ideas of *Bildung* and *Kultur*, with Weimar as their source, were transmitted to Western Europe and America by Benjamin Constant, Mme. de Staël, Coleridge, Carlyle, and Emerson.

Despite its high intellectual tone, Weimar was not

a musical centre until Liszt came there in 1848. In
the early years of the eighteenth century J. S. Bach
had been court organist and Kammermusikus there
from 1708 to 1717 but was only too glad to leave
for Köthen. Weimar's musical life was stagnant
during most of the century, for the Duchy had
suffered during the Seven Years' War, and largely
on that account a complete musical establishment
was impossible. From the mid-1750s to around 1770
Weimar could support only a wind ensemble
(*Harmoniemusik*), the typical music of the impecu-
nious court. Strings were added to this group
around 1770, but even in 1783 there were only a
dozen players in the orchestra; though the orchestra
at the end of the century was medium-sized by the
standards of the time, it had to be reinforced with
military bandsmen, students, and *Stadtmusikanten*.

Before 1783, musical drama in Weimar consisted
of amateur theatricals managed by Goethe in which
Corona Schröter, who came as court singer in 1776,
was the only professional; but by 1783 Bellomo's
troupe of actors and singers became semi-permanent
residents of Weimar, giving the duchy a repertoire
consisting mostly of Italian *opere buffe* and the lighter
Singspiele, although they performed Mozart's *Die
Entführung aus dem Serail* in 1785. Goethe assumed
the direction of the court theatre in 1791, retaining
many of Bellomo's singers, adding new ones, and
markedly raising the dramatic and musical standards
of performance and repertoire.

Unfortunately the musical directors in Weimar
were undistinguished even by the standards of the

time. Ernst Wilhelm Wolf, František Benda's son-
in-law, came in 1761 as musical director and died in
1792. He was followed by Johann Friedrich Kranz,
who had come to Weimar in 1766, left to study in
1781, and returned in 1789 as concertmaster of the
court orchestra and musical director of Bellomo's
theatre; subsequently he was made conductor of the
court opera in 1792 and Kapellmeister in 1799.
Whether he was the 'Cranz' who was studying violin
with Ignaz Fränzl and composition with Holzbauer
when Schiller met him in Mannheim is unknown,
and Schiller virtually ignored the man after showing
initial interest in him. After Kranz left Weimar in
1803, he was succeeded by Franz Seraph von
Destouches, who wrote most of the music for the
Weimar performances of Schiller's later dramas.
Not until Johann Nepomuk Hummel came in 1819
did a composer of stature settle in Weimar. At times
a few visiting virtuosi came through and gave
concerts, among them Ferdinand Fränzl; Ferdinand
Eck (subsequently Spohr's violin teacher), whom
Schiller recommended to Körner;[16] and the Pixis
brothers; Karl Stamitz lived and taught for a short
time in Jena; but because of the limited opportunities
famous performers did not settle in Weimar, thus
forcing the lovers of instrumental music to settle for
concerts of *Harmoniemusik* or a clarinet concerto
played by Destouches.

On the other hand, there was a lively 'do-it-your-
self' interest in *Hausmusik*, amateur performing of
technically easy literature, which one must understand, according to one of Schiller's leading biogra-

phers, fully to appreciate the domestic culture in
Germany at the end of the eighteenth and the beginning of the nineteenth centuries.[17] Many of the
members of the court circle in Weimar played instruments or sang, and Duchess Anna Amalia and Count
von Seckendorff even composed music.

The musical activities of many of the important
figures in Weimar remains to be fully investigated.
Wieland is said to have had a lively feeling for music,
but a study of his relationship to this art remains to
be written. Although much has been written about
Goethe's relationship to music, Herder had more
knowledge of this art, and his musical activities
included working with J. C. F. Bach at Bückeburg
and translating the texts of Handel's *Messiah* and
Alexander's Feast for performances in Weimar in
1780, yet only recently have scholars begun system-
atically to investigate the many contributions which
this versatile man made to the philosophy and
aesthetics of music. The dowager duchess Anna
Amalia, who presided over musical life in Weimar,
displayed considerable skill in composing and
appreciating music, for she wrote songs for Goethe's
Singspiele and treasured in her library the autograph
finale of Gluck's *Orfeo ed Euridice* and the manuscript
of Mozart's K. 450 piano concerto.

The Schlick family and Corona Schröter were
among Schiller's first musical friends in Weimar.
He enjoyed visiting Kammerherr von Einsiedel
because 'in [his] house I can hear music; a certain
Schlick comes and goes.' The Schlicks must have
been famous, for Schiller wrote Körner that he

probably knew them by reputation: 'he plays the cello excellently and [his wife] the violin.'[18]

Corona Schröter, as a professional among amateurs, made many important contributions to Weimar's musical life, among them singing the soprano solos in Herder's productions of Handel's oratorios and in Goethe's *Singspiele*. Her settings of some of Goethe's poems are quite charming considering their brevity and scope. After the court theatre was placed on a permanent basis in 1791 she retired from active singing and devoted herself mainly to training the young actors and coaching the singers. Schiller accompanied her to social gatherings and even played whist with her, but although she was quite impressed with him, he had initial reservations about her intellectual qualities:

> The exaggerated admiration of good minds has given her a better impression of herself than she would have pretended to, as she can maintain her self-confidence. I believe her proper merit is to oversee a household; to me she seems to have contentedly insipid ideas about art. Moreover, one is good and comfortable in her company, but goes away from her quiet and empty.[19]

Yet these initial opinions did not hinder a warmly cordial relationship. Two months later Schiller wrote that he was on the 'most charming terms' with her and that 'she has recently made me a present of her songs [probably the 'Fünf und Zwanzig Lieder' of 1786] and I of *Don Carlos* to her.'[20]

During Schiller's stay in Weimar two formal musical events customarily took place: a Sunday afternoon reception open to the nobility, followed by a concert and cards, and Anna Amalia's concert on Wednesday afternoons. During his first visit to Weimar the Duchess invited Schiller to attend a performance of one of her *Singspiele*, but Charlotte von Lengefeld (later his wife) advised him not to go because he had not received a formal invitation; Gotter later told him that he had behaved badly by not going. We know that Anna Amalia repeated the invitation, for Schiller wrote: 'This morning I have again received an invitation to tea, a concert, and supper with the Duchess.' He was not highly impressed with her:

> She herself has not captivated me . . . Her spirit is extremely narrow-minded, nothing interests her unless it is connected with sensual things; this [affects her] taste for music and painting and the like. She is herself a composer; Goethe's *Erwin und Elmire* has been set by her.[21]

Jena, where Schiller was professor of history from 1789 until his illness in 1791, boasted considerable musical activity. The University supported an active Collegium Musicum, an orchestra in which musically inclined students participated; although none of the programs given by this group before 1817 have been preserved, one can reasonably conjecture that the works of the composers of the Berlin and Mannheim symphonic schools and Haydn provided

most of the repertoire. That good local composers
were active there is shown by the so-called 'Jena'
symphony by Friedrich Witt which was attributed
to Beethoven for several years. In 1804 Jena was
said to have been second only to Leipzig in having
the best University music in Germany. No record
exists of Schiller's having attended any University
concerts, but the students customarily serenaded
with music and Schiller was thus greeted after his
famous inaugural lecture.

Several of his colleagues and friends there were
musical. He frequently attended concerts at Hufeland's home and heard *Don Giovanni* sung there.[22]
After he became ill, he was visited by J. B. Erhard,
who impressed him not only with his breadth of
learning and many talents but also his musicality.
Anton Thibaut, the connoisseur of sixteenth-century
music who was later to contribute markedly to the
reform of Catholic church music through his book
Über Reinheit der Tonkunst, taught in Jena between
1800 and 1805; Schiller knew him, received visits
from him, and was disappointed when he left Jena,
but there is no account of their holding conversations about music.

Schiller's wife provided throughout his career his
most intimate musical experiences. When he met
Charlotte von Lengefeld and her married sister
Karoline von Beulwitz in December of 1787 in
Rudolstadt, he was delighted: 'They play the piano
well, which made a lovely evening for me.'[23] With
his fortunes improved by his professorship at Jena

and an annual stipend from the Duke, and with
Karoline's subtle urgings, he proposed marriage,
was accepted, and was wed to Charlotte in Wenigen-
jena on 22 February 1790.

'Next week Lolo will start piano and voice study,'
Schiller wrote in describing how his new bride was
planning to improve her musical proficiency.[24] A
charming account by the Danish poet Jens Baggessen
shows how Charlotte used music to distract her
husband from the pain of a toothache:

> I noticed that he was suffering and requested him
> to take care of himself when his wife sat down at
> the piano to let [my wife] hear what she had re-
> cently learned. At this opportunity we talked
> about music, of which Schiller understood nothing
> at all but, as he said to me, had an extraordinary
> love for it.[25]

Charlotte's musical skill must have declined after the
birth of her first child, for five years after the wedding
Schiller wrote that he had no usable piano in his
home in Jena and that no one there could perform,
although Lotte did own a mandolin. Her singing
had also languished, for Schiller wrote Körner to
thank him for a group of songs: 'I would be able to
enjoy them fully if I could find someone who sings
very well,' and later, 'As much as our ladies like to
sing, they understand so little music.'[26] Yet a piano
must have been acquired between 1795 and 1800,
for Lotte's cousin Christiane von Wurmb said that a
piano, which Amy Fay called a 'tiny little piano'

during her visit to Weimar in 1871, was situated in a room adjoining Schiller's study.[27]

Karoline von Beulwitz (later von Wolzogen), apparently more musical or at least more articulate about music than her sister Charlotte, puts in her biography of Schiller much information about his musical preferences. Music was an important aid to his creative imagination:

> Schiller loved music very much and liked to have it in an adjoining room when he walked up and down in his study and gave himself up to a poetic mood. This influenced my sister to take further instruction in piano playing. The song by Gluck, "Einen Bach, der fliesst," gave Schiller the most agreeable fantasies.*

She further commented that 'Music . . . affected him mysteriously; he had never practiced it, but he said that it agreeably affected his poetic moods.'[28] Charlotte later remembered his fondness for vocal music:

> Karoline's [Schiller's daughter] voice is so lovely and touching that I often think how her dear father would have been inspired to many noble, beautiful, and elevated thoughts if he could have heard his daughter's voice. During his work he loved to hear song from a distance.[29]

* O. W. Neighbour of the British Museum has identified this ariette as 'Un ruisselet, bien clair' from *La Rencontre imprévue*, first published in German in 1772.

Music played a part in the intimate pictures of Schiller *en pantoufles*: listening to music while sitting under
the trees and drinking beer during his convalescence
in Karlsbad, having a guitar made for Körner (his
son Theodor, the poet, took this instrument into
battle in 1813 where he was killed), or enjoying a
serenade given him by students from the University
of Halle; the musicians who accompanied the
students, when asked to play the melodies of Schiller's songs, knew only 'An die Freude' and thus
played this one piece repeatedly.[30]

Christiane von Wurmb often sang and played for
Schiller during her visit to Weimar. Frequently she
would sit in a room adjoining Schiller's study and
play Lotte's piano when he called out 'Einen Marsch,
Christel! Einen Marsch!'[31] In her reminiscences of
her stay in Weimar she mentioned some of the poet's
excellent advice to her; when she expressed the desire
to sing like her teacher Karoline Jagemann, he said:

> The admiration of an art, talent, or what it may be,
> generally leads to the fine wish also to possess it.
> Through good training this feeling is surely a
> great means of elevating human powers to per-
> fection.

And when she later told him that she was afraid to
sing in public in Rudolstadt, he gently replied in
words that every aspiring musician should know:

> Serious good will is a great, the most beautiful
> characteristic quality of the spirit. Success is
> bestowed by a higher, invisible hand. Only the
> intention gives worth to the expenditure of powers.

Thus we raise ourselves above the praise and blame of men.[32]

When Christel left for Berlin, Schiller warmly recommended her to Zelter.

Karoline von Wolzogen gives the last account of Schiller's love of music:

A few weeks before his last illness he heard Mlle. Schmalz sing at my home; her soulful singing moved him deeply. She sang the lovely aria from Zingarelli's *Romeo e Giulietta*, 'Ombra adorata aspetta,' and Schiller said to me, 'never has a song touched me in this manner.' It seemed as if [his approaching death] had sharpened all the senses of his spirit and feelings.[33]

Mozart's Requiem was performed at Schiller's funeral in 1805.[34]

A little-known aspect of Schiller's relationship with music was his attitude toward writing opera librettos. *Semele*, as we have seen, was intended as an opera but its author later repudiated it. Although opera as an art-form repelled him between 1784 and 1796, and throughout his career he rebuffed composers who sought librettos from him, he made three dramatic sketches which can be considered at least potential librettos.

All the information we have about the earliest of these is a letter to Huber in 1786 in which Schiller remarked that he had written two arias and a trio

and had given them to a composer whose name he
did not mention:

> I hope, and this is my blessed conviction, that
> the music will turn out a bit worse than the arias,
> and these are certainly bad. In the meantime there
> is an opera under my wig, and I am doing it with
> the intention of – scribbling in order to learn.[35]

Though not interested in writing operas himself,
Körner repeatedly sought to interest Schiller in
collaborating with distinguished composers. His
first venture, in 1787, was to have the poet write a
libretto for Naumann:

> Naumann spoke to me again about an opera which
> you are going to do for him. In the autumn he is
> going to Berlin and intends to discuss a national
> opera with the King. He will summon all his
> powers to give the music a proper character which
> will be distinguished through truth and dignity.
> For him, Klopstock's plays are too sterile for the
> theatre. From you he expects more knowledge of
> the theatre, less crudeness in the versification, and
> similar terseness in the dialogue. He spoke with
> spirit and dignity on the matter, so that he stands
> very high in my favor. What do you say to this
> idea?

Schiller was also invited to come to Dresden during
the summer to discuss the project personally with
Naumann, but nothing further happened.[36]

Also in 1787 Schiller became interested in Wieland's *Oberon* and considered it 'a splendid subject for music.' He hoped that Kranz, who had just returned from his studies, would be a suitable composer and planned to give him the libretto. Körner dissuaded him from this project with the words 'Why not find a subject yourself?' and stated that he would be better able to create an effectively unified dramatic work if he did not have to work out single pieces under a musician's guidance. Naumann was again suggested as a composer.[37]

Two possible attempts at opera by Schiller can be dated from the late 1790s. A sketch for one on the Orpheus legend is apparently based on the second act of Calzabigi's libretto for Gluck's *Orfeo ed Euridice*. The principal departure from this model was Schiller's having Orpheus sing a 'Hymn to Life' before the spirits in Hades. All that remains of the hymn are notes made for the topics of the first three stanzas.

Storz states that the sketch for *Rosamund oder die Braut der Höhle* was an operatic attempt and that two versions may have been intended, one for the stage and one for the opera house. He also believes that Schiller was approaching Romantic opera, especially Mozart's *Die Zauberflöte*;[38] this is most evident in Schiller's directions for the décor of the finale, which includes wild animals, columns, harpies, birds, temples, gardens, palaces, and ghosts. The closest specific connection with opera in *Rosamund* is Schiller's note about 'through what means Rosamund's role can win favor. As a *singer* it can happen

only through song, as an *actress* — . . .'[39] All else that
exists of the abortive *Rosamund* is an incomplete
ballad with several stanzas missing.

Zumsteeg hoped to induce Schiller to write a
libretto for him. In a rather pathetic letter he appealed to his old school friend: 'My most ardent
wish is still to receive an opera from you. Is this
[wish] never to be satisfied?' Zumsteeg offered him
the choice of plot and its realization, but preferred
something 'heroisch-komisch;' the only essential
requirement was two finales. Zumsteeg closed his
letter by asking: 'Perhaps you would do something
sooner for your friend than for the composer,' and
mentioned the success of his opera *Die Geisterinsel*
to prove that he was skilled in this kind of composition.[40]   Since none of the letters Schiller wrote
to Zumsteeg after 1794 have been preserved, we
have no way of knowing how this request was
declined.

In 1801 Körner made a last attempt to interest
Schiller in opera by sending him a sketch of *Alfred*,
the music to which was to be a series of 'musical
paintings' and written by a new arrival in Dresden,
'a not unskilled composer, [Ferdinando] Paër, who
must write two operas a year.' Schiller suggested
that Kotzebue write the libretto but doubted that it
would be effective, and Körner did not relish the
idea of collaborating with him.[41]

Probably as an emissary from Bernhard Anselm
Weber, the music student Schlömilch came to Weimar from Berlin in 1803 to inquire about Schiller's
interest in writing an opera libretto but was rebuffed:

'This is not my field; go to Kotzebue or Goethe,'
and in the following year Weber's personal request
for a libretto was refused.[42]

Schiller stated the real reason for refusing to become an opera librettist in a letter to Goethe about
the latter's sketches for a sequel to *Die Zauberflöte*:

> If you do not have a very skillful and popular
> composer . . . I fear that you are putting yourself
> in danger of having an ungrateful audience, for in
> the performance itself no libretto will redeem an
> opera if the music is not successful; frequently the
> poet is also blamed for the failure.[43]

And this is further confirmed in a letter to Iffland
shortly after Schiller rejected Weber's offer of
collaboration on an opera:

> [The secretary of the theatre directorate in Berlin]
> has spoken to me about a grand opera. For a long
> time I have also had a desire for such an under-
> taking, but if on my part I break my head to do the
> right thing, I would also like to be certain that the
> composer is competent. A tragedy can amount
> to something independent of the talent of the
> actor; an opera is nothing if it is not played or
> sung.[44]

Schiller refused to write a libretto because he
evidently was not satisfied with the operatic abilities
of any of the composers whom he knew, even one
with an international reputation like Naumann. He

may also have been influenced by the fate of Goethe's
Singspiele which had been set to music by such
amateur composers as Duchess Anna Amalia and
Kammerherr von Seckendorff, and thus enjoyed
from a musical standpoint a renown restricted to the
environs of Weimar. Between the death of Mozart
and the later works of Carl Maria von Weber
German opera (with the sole exception of *Fidelio* by
Beethoven which was chiefly influenced by French
models) was in a state of stagnation, with its leading
composers merely minor figures. The centre of
operatic gravity had shifted to France with the
'rescue operas' of Grétry, Cherubini, Dalayrac,
Lesueur, and Méhul, any of whom in their better
moments would have written music which could
have complemented Schiller's inspiration, for their
music, which derived from Gluck and the musical
Sturm und Drang, shares the elevation, the attempts
at the sublime, and even the occasional elements of
bombast in Schiller's poetic language. Unfortunately Schiller knew Dalayrac and Grétry only by
their lighter *opéras comiques*, probably never heard
any rescue operas with the possible exception of
Cherubini's *Les deux journées*, and although his dramas were known in France since the first performance of *Die Räuber* in Paris in 1792, there is no
record of his having been approached by any French
composer. Schiller's influence on the opera libretto
was not felt until the nineteenth century.

We know that Schiller never played a musical instrument, although he enjoyed instrumental music and

knew how instruments were built. Whether he ever sang, however, has been a topic for controversy since his death. The dispute was opened immediately after his demise by C. W. Oemler, who quoted Charlotte as having said that he 'sang, after a long pause, [a] verse from Klopstock's ode ... with a tone that made my inmost soul tremble.' Schiller's brother-in-law Reinwald scornfully attacked this statement two years later:

> Schiller never sang, at least not in his later life, in any case not as late as Klopstock's death [1803]. He had no voice, he lacked the ability to control his voice, and absolutely in his later years his chest was so weak that only with great difficulty could he declaim his own verses, and he is said to have sung so that he moved the listener! This is quite a joke!

And Charlotte remarked on another occasion that her husband never sang.[45]

Many of those who knew Schiller gave accounts of the difficulty he had with his speaking voice. Friedrich Scharffenstein remembered that at the Karlsschule his voice was 'shrill and disagreeable' and that he could not control it; this would have prevented his becoming even a 'tolerable actor.' Baggessen stated that in 1790 Schiller had to hold a handkerchief over his mouth and could speak only with difficulty. Such words as 'weak, unmanly, almost quavering,' and 'dull' are found in comments on Schiller's voice after his illness forced him to give up lecturing in public.[46] His problems in speaking would have been considerably multiplied in singing.

On the other hand Johann Heinrich Voss the younger, a close friend of Schiller's whose remarks can be considered reliable, gave an eyewitness account of his singing:

> We sat in the corner close to the room where the faro bank was located and caroused. We drank his health aloud and clinked glasses. Schiller was so animated that he struck up his 'So leben wir,' at which some students who were present were highly astonished. Afterwards four or five of us joined in another song and altogether we drank eleven bottles of champagne.[47]

If Schiller did sing at all, it must have been at the expense of considerable physical effort and even discomfort, took place only at moments of strong emotional stress or well-lubricated conviviality, and was so rare as to arouse astonishment and to make a lasting impression on those who were present, but his singing could not have been a significant aesthetic experience.

Schiller was one of the first intellectual leaders whose musical tastes were based on personal feelings and abstract judgments rather than on experience as a performer of music or as a student of the technical and theoretical side of this art. In the various communities where he lived, their days of musical glory had passed (Ludwigsburg, Stuttgart, Leipzig, Dresden) or their musical horizons were restricted and provincial (Bauerbach, Jena, Weimar). His musical pilgrimage was nevertheless an orderly process, displaying his development from his childhood when he was impressed with operatic spectacle, through his young manhood when he was hypnotized by dreamy clavier playing, to his maturity when music played an important part in his daily life and he made significant use of this art in his dramas, poems, and philosophical essays.

II. MUSIC IN SCHILLER'S DRAMATIC WORKS

A forceful and effective use of incidental music is characteristic of Schiller's dramas, the works through which he is best known today. Schiller can be considered superior to Goethe and surpassed only by Shakespeare in his employment of music as an important dramatic adjunct.

Schiller was not acquainted with the mediaeval liturgical drama, the intermedii of the Italian court theatres of the Renaissance, or the school dramas of the Jesuits, all of which contained varying amounts of incidental music. The fundamental sources of his dramatic use of music are the histories and tragedies of Shakespeare. Elizabethan drama was an integration of all the arts, not only literature but also poetry, music, and dance. Shakespeare did not employ song and dance in his histories and tragedies to the extent that he did in his comedies, but many effects that Schiller later used are in Shakespeare's plays: distorted songs in *Romeo and Juliet* (II, 4) and *2 Henry IV* (II, 4); dance music (the ball in *Romeo and Juliet*); banquet music (*Macbeth*, I, 7); marches and flourishes in virtually every drama; and even the melodrama, music as background to spoken words, in *Richard II*, v, 5.

The Restoration theatre made an even greater use of incidental music than the Elizabethan stage. The music ranged from drum beats which was the complete orchestral music for the poorer sort of 'Strowling' players to the elaborate use of soloists, choruses, and full orchestra in Purcell's incidental music to Dryden's *King Arthur* and *The Indian Queen*. As the following anonymous poem of 1742 attests, a lavish use of incidental music continued in English drama during the eighteenth century:

> In former times no Orchestra was known
> But thrice before the Play a Horn was blown.
> But since the Æra of the Restoration
> The Playhouses grew politer with the Nation;
> Drums, Kettle-drums and Trumpets, Hautboys,
>   Flutes,
> Violoncellos, Violins, and Lutes,
> Concerts, Concertos, Overtures, and Airs,
> Are now all used to introduce the Players.[1]

The wandering troupes of English comedians, with their musical entr'actes and divertissements, most strongly influenced the employment of incidental music in German drama. The music included accompaniment for festive meals, songs with instrumental support, and additional music to express certain moods, such as the sad music added to the oath of revenge in *Titus Andronicus* or the mausoleum scene in *Romeo and Juliet*. Around 1700 the English dramas and comedies in Germany were affected by a variety of influences: Baroque opera with its machines; Italian operas and pastorals; Spanish baroque drama; French *comédies*, *comédies larmoyantes*, and *opéras comiques;* German art drama; and Jesuit school drama. Pickelhering, the clown, roamed freely through these literary agglomerations, and music was an integral part of edifying spectacle and comic entertainment as well as a filler of such prosaic functions as getting actors on and off stage and concealing the noise of the machines.

Johann Adolf Scheibe began the reformation of dramatic incidental music in Germany. His basic criterion was that the music should be appropriate to the situation portrayed or to be portrayed on the stage. The overtures to the comedies and tragedies should be different, with the overtures for tragedies 'splendid, fiery, and spirited,' whereas those for the comedies should be 'free, flowing, and sometimes scherzo-like.' The overture should be related to the first scene of the drama, but special attention should be given to the main character and the basic theme of the play. The entr'actes should be suitable both to the closing scene of the preceding act and the opening scene of the next act, even if it meant having an entr'acte written in two sections (the intermezzo from Mendelssohn's music to *A Midsummer Night's Dream*, to be played between the second and third acts, is an excellent illustration). The closing music should correspond with the final scene, for is it not ridiculous when the hero dies in a tragic manner and a lively and merry sinfonia immediately ensues? The instrumentation of the overture should be strong and full, and it was not good to have too much changing of the instrumentation in the entr'actes. Finally, each drama should have its own incidental music.[2]

Johann Christoph Gottsched, the theatrical reformer of the first half of the eighteenth century, was quite interested in music and a study of his relationship to this art is needed. His remarks about incidental music generally agree with those of Scheibe.

Gottsched believed that the music should agree with the drama but proposed 'all kinds of merry pieces' as entr'actes and even recommended performing between the acts cantatas which would reflect 'on the preceding material and contain moral observations thereon.'[3]

The dramas of Gotthold Ephraim Lessing are considered to be the watershed between the viable German theatre and the drama of purely historical interest. He did not specify incidental music in any of his plays, probably to ensure their being performed on as many stages as possible, yet Burney described a performance of *Emilia Galotti* in 1772 in which the overture and 'act-tunes' by Haydn, Hoffmann, and Vanhal were 'well-performed and had an admirable effect;' evidence that music could be used in these dramas but its employment was not mandatory.[4]

Lessing's *Hamburgische Dramaturgie* (1767) is the most important literary work of the eighteenth century in which a discussion of dramatic incidental music is contained. He makes many extensive quotations from Scheibe's treatise but adds significant observations of his own. The orchestra should perform the same function in the play as the chorus does in Greek drama. He differs from Scheibe's views on entr'acte music by stating that the music should reflect the character of only the preceding act; since the tragic poet loves the unexpected, the music should not prematurely reveal the dramatist's surprises. As an illustration of good incidental music, he gives a detailed analysis of Agricola's

music to Voltaire's *Semiramis*. It is therefore sur-
prising to encounter in Robertson's study of the
Hamburgische Dramaturgie the remark: 'What [Les-
sing] has to say about the employment of music in
the theatre is not of much consequence.' [6]

A drama quite interesting from the standpoint of
its music is the tragedy *Olint und Sophronie* by Johann
Friedrich Cronegk, who died in 1758 before finishing
his masterpiece. Each of the three completed acts
of the drama ends with a chorus. That these choruses
were intended to be sung rather than spoken is
shown by such musical directions as 'whole chorus,'
'recitative by a single person, 'and 'arioso.' An
antiphonal chorus concludes the second act and
soloists join the chorus for the finale to Act III.
Although Lessing devotes the first part of his
Hamburgische Dramaturgie to a criticism of this
tragedy, he does not mention its use of music.

A great increase in the use of incidental music in
Germany began during the 1760s. Evans has advanced the theory that since in most courts and cities
the same theatre was used for both opera and drama,
and since an orchestra was permanently employed,
dramatists had more incentive to use incidental
music so that the orchestra members would not be
both idle and paid on the nights when plays were
given. [7] The orchestras in the eighteenth century
were not only concert organizations but also played
for dances, meals, and open-air parties; performing
music at plays was only one of the many duties of
the orchestra musicians. The period between 1750
and 1780 is one of steady expansion in the size and

number of orchestras in Germany, and the mere availability of an orchestra of some kind in every community which supported a theatre is one of the principal reasons for the efflorescence of dramatic music.

The Shakespeare revival in Germany during the second half of the eighteenth century also advanced the cause of incidental music. The translations used were not those of the comedians, but those of Wieland (who translated 22 of Shakespeare's plays between 1762 and 1766) as revised by Eschenbach in 1775. As we have seen, Shakespeare used incidental music as an integral part of all his dramas except the farces.

The melodrama strongly influenced the incidental music of the eighteenth century. Rousseau's *Pygmalion*, first performed in 1770, was set to music twice in 1772 by German composers; the most popular melodrama was Georg Benda's *Ariadne auf Naxos*, a work which Schiller admired. In both the eighteenth and nineteenth centuries melodrama was used in operas as well as in plays to serve as a relief from song or speech and to underscore striking dramatic situations. A melodrama in German drama occurs as early as 1768 in the closing scene of Gerstenberg's *Ugolino;* the stage directions specify that 'after [Ugolino] has played some chords on the lute, a gentle sad music is heard;' the music continues through the dialogue between Ugolino and Anselmo and at the end of the drama 'concludes in an exalted manner.'

The dramatic ballet and the reformed *opera seria*

were also important influences on dramatic music.
Noverre, the choreographer who is regarded as the
virtual creator of the dramatic ballet, was in Karl
Eugen's service in Württemberg; although he had
been dismissed during Schiller's childhood, his ideas
were retained in the ballet instruction given at the
Karlsschule. The dramatic ballet, of which Gluck's
Don Juan is the first major example, does not consist
of dances which are independent and an end in themselves but is a dramatic idea requiring the equal
participation of music, pantomime, and spectacle.

Although Gluck is generally credited with achieving greater unity of music with drama in the opera,
Jommelli and Traëtta also brought these elements
into close co-ordination, and we have already seen
the admiration (and in *Semele*, even emulation) that
the young Schiller showed for Jommelli's operas.
An examination of Jommelli's *Fetonte* (1768), published in the *Denkmäler der Tonkunst in Deutschland*, will
show the importance of spectacle, elaborate stage
directions and ballets, and the use of incidental
music to effect changes of scene.

Schiller was also strongly impressed during his
youth by Holzbauer's opera *Günther von Schwarzburg*
and praised it in 1785: '. . . the crowd was larger
than usual. The effect? When a bungling performance can be forgotten amid pomp and musical
beauties, extraordinary.'[8] The opera is a very
dramatic work and the libretto contains many stage
directions which are often accompanied by lengthy
ritornels; one of 46 measures of allegro moderato
(with oboe concertato) precedes the Pfalzgräfin's

aria in Act I. Much scope is afforded pomp and pageantry, and the triumphal march in Act II can be regarded as a precursor not only of the coronation march in *Die Jungfrau von Orleans* but also of similar scenes in the nineteenth-century grand opera from Spontini's *La Vestale* to Verdi's *Aida*.

The generation of dramatists which came after Lessing and are generally called the 'Stürmer und Dränger' made an extensive use of music in their plays for dramatic effect and character portrayal. Klinger often used clavier playing on the stage, Goethe specified songs in *Götz von Berlichingen* and the *Urfaust*, Maler Müller called for an elaborate onstage serenade in *Doktor Fausts Leben und Tod*, and Lenz employed lute lessons, violin playing, vocal and orchestral concerts, and distorted songs in his dramas. The Stürmer und Dränger strove to depict life realistically on the stage and thus used music not only to intensify dramatic action but also portrayed amateur and even professional musicians. Theory lagged behind practice, for most of the treatises on drama written during this period omitted discussion of incidental music. The best account of the effect of dramatic music is in Goethe's novel of theatrical life, *Wilhelm Meister*. The actor Laertes speaks:

> I don't consider myself either a great actor or singer, but I do know that when the music guides the movements of the body, gives them life, and at the same time prescribes the meter; when declamation and expression are conveyed to me by the composer, then I am another man than I am when

in a prose drama everything has already been created; I must combine measure and declamation first, [and] every fellow actor disturbs me.

Schiller himself made a few observations on incidental music. In one of his earliest essays on the drama he complained about its inappropriate use: even when a production was effective, 'soon a noisy allegro sweeps these gentle feelings away.'[9] During his 'anti-opera' period, which lasted between 1784 and 1796, he glowingly described the absence of 'spectacle and operatic décor' in his projected *Don Carlos*, and in his review of Goethe's *Egmont* he sharply criticized the use of music in its ending:

> ... in the middle of a very realistic and stirring situation we are transported through a *salto mortale* into an operatic world to *see* a dream.

He also used such expressions as 'ridiculous ... the author has sinned against nature and truth' in describing a scene which closely resembles the dream in *Cymbeline* (v, 5).[10] Yet despite his previous criticism Schiller retained this scene when he adapted *Egmont* for the Weimar stage, and in his notes for the unfinished portions of his incomplete tragedy *Demetrius* he planned to have the spirit of Axinia appear to Romanow in his prison cell.

In the year of Schiller's death Tolev wrote an interesting essay on incidental music for the *Allgemeine musikalische Zeitung*, the leading musical periodical in Germany. One of the chief purposes of

incidental music was to make the audience attentive
and to keep them from being bored between the acts.
Theatregoers had to wait before the play began;
therefore why not a little concert? Vocal music in
the entr'actes would be too much like opera, but a
good effect could be achieved through instrumental
renditions of songs from the drama. Tolev repeated
the common complaint about the use of merry
music after the final scene of a tragedy but quoted as
an extenuation of this practice the words of a theatre
manager: '*Mein Gott*, tragic things in succession
exhaust the public too much, therefore a rondo is a
real relief.'[11]

Among the most important composers during the
eighteenth century of incidental music were Johann
André (*The Barber of Seville*, *Hamlet*, *King Lear*) and
Johann Friedrich Reichardt, whose music to *Macbeth*
was the most widely circulated incidental music of
this period. Although Schiller was a personal enemy
of Reichardt, he nevertheless esteemed his music for
Macbeth and recommended that all of the music
except the overture be used for his adaptation of
Shakespeare's drama.[12]

Music which accompanies the basically spoken drama
fills a variety of functions. Signals, fanfares, and
marches serve an ancillary purpose often essential
for the full understanding of the action. Songs,
choruses, and dance music can amplify what takes
place on the stage, provide relief from the steady
movement of a tightly-knit drama, or can delineate
character. Music can intensify the impact of the

drama, animate the action, or create such atmospheres as those of mystery and awe. Music in the drama can, in Morgan's words, 'do something of a dramatic nature which words could not have done so well, if at all.'[13] These different purposes of incidental music occur in Schiller's dramas.

Music as pure sound effect occurs frequently in Schiller's dramas. Trumpet signals are often used in military scenes, and in Mannheim two trumpeters were employed solely to play the battle signals in *Die Räuber*. Horns announce the hunt in *Wilhelm Tell* (III, 2, 3) and arrivals in *Die Braut von Messina*, and although there is no specific stage direction, the dialogue calls for them in *Maria Stuart* (III, 1). Such devices are a means of dramatic economy, implying offstage action through music without the necessity for either extensive verbal explanation or crowd scenes on the stage.

Schiller acquired from the Elizabethan dramatists the device of using a flourish for ceremonial scenes. In his adaptation of *Macbeth* the acclamation 'Heil dem König Schottlands!' (V, 14) is followed by a flourish exactly as in Shakespeare's original drama (V, 8), but in *Fiesko* the flourish is used without dramatic sense, for when the conspirators toast 'The Republic!' a flourish is played. 'Drums, flight, and pursuit,' a common stage direction in Shakespeare's histories, accompany the combat between Johanna and Montgomery in *Die Jungfrau von Orleans;* drums help create an atmosphere of tumult in the revolution scenes of the last act of *Fiesko;* and a drumbeat announces the erection of Gessler's cap in *Wilhelm Tell*

(1, 3). In this same drama the 'ranz des vaches,' played on alphorns, proclaims an assembly of the Swiss. Among the most effective percussive sound effects are the scene in Schiller's adaptation of Gozzi's *Turandot* (1, 3) where the placing of a newly severed head atop the city gate is accompanied by 'out-of-tune drums,' possibly timpani in augmented fourths (which may have been a precedent for the use of this effect in the opening of Act II of Beethoven's *Fidelio*), and the 'warlike instruments' to accompany the cries of 'Vivat Ferdinandus!' with which the Imperialist troops drown out Wallenstein's attempts to address them (*Wallensteins Tod*, III, 21).

Knudsen's statement that Schiller's characters frequently refer to music before it is played is true only of the first act of *Fiesko*.[14] The battle signals and flourishes in Schiller's dramas occur where there is a definite cue for which music would be appropriate, but music is most frequently used at the beginning of an act or a new scene where there is a change of stage setting, or as a musical cue which is commented on after the music is played. An illustration of this is the 'martial music from afar' in *Die Piccolomini* (1, 2), which Illo explains:

> Das sind sie!
> Die Wachen salutieren – Dies Signal
> Bedeutet uns, die Fürstin sei herein.

The march is the principal kind of extended composition which Schiller specified for his stage music.

In Act IV of *Die Jungfrau von Orleans* the coronation march sounds in the distance at the opening of Scene 4 as Johanna's family assembles during this and the following scene; Scene 6 is entirely given over to the march, which begins with 'fifers and oboists' and includes even choirboys with censers. In traditional performances of this march the musicians in the orchestra play in alternation with the musicians on the stage.[15] The march ends when the procession enters the cathedral and the doors are closed.

Other examples of independent marches are the funeral march for Don Manuel in *Die Braut von Messina* and the marches in *Turandot* (II, 2, 4; V, 1), the directions for which Schiller took directly from the translation of Gozzi's play made between 1777 and 1779 by August Clemens Werthes. In *Fiesko* (V, 11) Schiller merely specifies a victory march with 'drums, horns, and oboes.' The 'Pappenheimer March' in *Wallensteins Tod* and the wedding march in *Wilhelm Tell* are of such dramatic significance that they will be discussed later in the chapter.

Dance music is occasionally used in Schiller's dramas. It serves as a background to the convivial and conspiratorial scenes in the first act of *Fiesko*, with a 'noisy allegro' as a transition to Scene 5 where the setting is changed to a large room filled with merrymakers. One of the comic scenes in *Wallensteins Lager* occurs when 'miners enter and play a waltz, first slowly and then with increasing speed.' Several soldiers choose partners and the First Jäger, pursuing a camp-follower, collides with a Capuchin friar who then upbraids the soldiers for their revelry.

Songs and choruses in the spoken drama may seem to intrude on the atmosphere of realism and to complicate the business of selecting casts. Dalberg omitted the songs from the first performance of *Die Räuber* but restored them after Schiller tactfully asked how Dalberg could 'unhappily eliminate the poetic portion of the drama in the . . . lyrical interludes.'[16] Although no song is written for Princess Eboli in *Don Carlos*, the stage directions (II, 7) require her to play the lute and to sing. Concerning this Schiller wrote:

> Can the actress to whom you are assigning [the role of] Princess Eboli sing an aria tolerably well? It is called for in the play, and if it is not possible I must make some changes.

And he also insisted that the actress portraying Thekla in *Die Piccolomini* must be able to sing.[17]

In most of the German theatres of the time actors and actresses were used in opera (especially *Singspiele*) and singers had to appear in plays. Goethe engaged his actors in Weimar for their vocal as well as dramatic abilities and in Mannheim even famous actresses had to participate in operatic productions. The actress for whom Schiller wrote his principal feminine roles from *Die Piccolomini* through *Wilhelm Tell* was Karoline Jagemann, renowned both as actress and singer. Schiller effectively utilized both her musical and dramatic talents: 'I have calculated on Thekla's part being played by Jagemann, and have given her a song to sing.'[18] Her contract in Weimar required her to undertake the first or second female singing roles and to act in plays 'from time to time,' and her voice has been described as 'artistically developed, charming, and sweet.'[19] From the nature of the operatic roles she performed in Weimar, she must have been a lyric soprano.

The songs in Schiller's dramas are:

Die Räuber
> Hektors Abschied: Willst dich,
>> Hektor (Amalia)
> Schön wie Engel (Amalia)
> Räuberlied: Karessieren, sauffen, balgen (chorus with strophes sung by individual robbers)
> Römerlied: Sei willkommen, friedliche Gefilde (Karl)

Wallensteins Lager
> Rekrutenlied: Trommeln und Pfeifen (recruit)
> Reiterlied: Wohl auf, Kameraden (chorus with strophes sung by individual soldiers).

Die Piccolomini
> Der Eichwald brauset (Thekla)

Macbeth
> Verschwunden ist die finstre Nacht (Porter)

Wilhelm Tell
> Es lächelt der See (fisher-boy, shepherd, chamois hunter)
> Mit dem Pfeil, dem Bogen (Walther)
> Rasch tritt der Tod (Barmherzige Brüder)

An unspecified song by Princess Eboli in *Don Carlos* and a funeral anthem for Don Manuel at the end of *Die Braut von Messina* are also required.

Most of the songs and choruses are used for stage settings or for characterization. Typical illustrations of the former are Amalia's 'Schön wie Engel' or the song with variations, 'Es lächelt der See,' which provides a peacefully serene opening for *Wilhelm Tell*. Many examples of song as characterization can be found – Amalia's sentimentality, Thekla's sadness, Spiegelberg's villainy, and Karl Moor's sensitive, troubled spirit are all mirrored in their songs. The choruses in *Die Räuber* and *Wallensteins Lager* aptly depict on one hand the brawling, undisciplined robbers and on the other the martial joys of soldiering; in addition, the 'Räuberlied' effectively sets the atmosphere to open the change of scene in the middle of Act iv and the 'Reiterlied' is an effective 'production number' on which to bring down the curtain. Walther's 'Mit dem Pfeil, dem Bogen' is a master-stroke of characterization; the song not only depicts the boy's innocence but its opening lines serve as a link with the ensuing scene where Gessler orders Tell to shoot the apple off his son's head.

Little use is made of music for music's sake or as a diversion. The porter's song in Schiller's adaptation of *Macbeth* was written to replace the low comedy in the original drama (ii, 3), whereas the chorus of the Barmherzige Brüder in *Wilhelm Tell* is, as Silz remarks, 'plainly a substitute for a Greek chorus and an effective finale to one of Schiller's most effective stage scenes.'[20]

The melodrama, Schiller's most effective atmospheric device, is reserved only for telling dramatic moments. The opening scene of Act iv of *Die*

Jungfrau von Orleans consists of Johanna's monologue
which is accompanied by 'flutes and oboes' behind
the scene; the music is later to become a 'tender,
touching melody' and only 'flutes' are to be used at
the end of her soliloquy. One writer has suggested
that the music for this melodrama should be a
continuation of the preceding entr'acte.[21] The
funeral anthem for Don Manuel in *Die Braut von
Messina* is the background music for Don Cesar's
speech before his suicide. Thekla's monologue in
Die Piccolomini (III, 9) is accompanied at the end by
the banquet music played at a distance; it continues
as an entr'acte and into the fourth act, when the
curtain rises on the banquet hall where the music is
played onstage by bandsmen from Terzky's regi-
ment.

Although there are no directions for music, some
of Schiller's spoken scenes would be very effective
as melodramas. Golther believed that Schiller
probably intended to have offstage hunting music
accompany the dialogue between Maria and Hannah
(*Maria Stuart*, III, 1), especially since Maria mentions
the sound of horns, and Burdach and Clark both
point out the operatic nature and conception of
Beatrice's entrance in *Die Braut von Messina*, which
was later set as an operatic scene by Franz von Hol-
stein in 1877.[22]

Schiller sometimes used music as a background
for dramatic action. This is most evident in *Fiesko*,
where dance music behind the scenes is to begin as
soon as the overture is finished, and in Act IV Fiesko
assembles the conspirators at a play which he is

giving for Doria's supporters; the overture to the play provides a background for the gathering of the conspirators, the Moor's treason, Fiesko's renunciation of Julia, and the decision to attack the Doge's forces.

In two of his later dramas Schiller employed this device with consummate mastery. At the close of the third act of *Wallensteins Tod* Max is held as a hostage in order to secure the loyalty of his troops, but they have just shouted Wallenstein down when he attempted to address them. Wallenstein, broken by this rebuff, enters and offers Max his liberty. As he orders Max and Thekla to part for the last time, the orchestra softly plays the Pappenheimer March as a group of cuirassiers files onstage. The music grows louder as Max bids farewell to his beloved and his fellow-officers. As he is led away by the cuirassiers, 'the music becomes overpowering and swells to a full war march which continues throughout the interval between the third and fourth acts,' a direction which appears in the Stuttgart and Berlin manuscripts and Coleridge's translation but is absent from both the SA and *Nationalausgabe* editions.

The wedding march in Act IV of *Wilhelm Tell* is similarly effective. The 'sprightly music' offstage begins during Tell's monologue, stops when Armgard pleads with Gessler for her husband's liberty, resumes (but more softly) during Gessler's angry ranting, and grows louder as the procession approaches and Tell kills Gessler. Gessler's lieutenant Harras orders the music stopped: 'Are the people mad that they make music to a murder?'

One of Schiller's most powerful scenes contains an abortive use of music. In *Wallensteins Tod* (III, 4) Thekla has learned that her father is in disfavor at the Imperial court and is urged by her aunt to use Max's love for her as a means of securing his adherence to Wallenstein's faction. She is extremely agitated when Wallenstein enters, asks her to sing, and hands her a zither. In the most effective versions the orchestra then plays a ritornel for a song. Thekla 'holds the instrument with a trembling hand, her soul is extremely agitated, and at the moment when she is supposed to sing, throws the instrument away and rapidly exits.'

Occasionally Schiller specified musical finales to his dramas. In *Wallensteins Lager* the curtain is to descend before the conclusion of the 'Reiterlied,' and in the last act of *Wilhelm Tell* the directions state 'while the music comes in again at a rapid tempo, the curtain falls.' In his revision of *Egmont* Schiller is rather prosaic; whereas Goethe's original version ended with a 'victory symphony,' his version merely calls for a continuation of the martial music which accompanied Egmont's dream.

The musical possibilities in *Die Braut von Messina* are more interesting than the specifications for music in this drama, which resembles a Greek tragedy in its use of the chorus. In his preface to the drama Schiller stated that his precedents were Greek tragedy and some of Shakespeare's plays. He considered the chorus not as an individual but as a group which would express itself about the past and future; on distant times and peoples, especially on the human element; and would draw conclusions on the grand outcome of life and the teachings of wisdom, achieving this effect 'with the full power of imagination, with a daring lyrical freedom which moves about the peaks of human affairs with the steps of the gods . . . accompanied by the entire sensuous power of rhythm and music in tones and movement.'[23] By 1802 Schiller was also acquainted with the impression that could be created by choral scenes through his knowledge of the operas of Jommelli, Holzbauer, Mozart (*Die Zauberflöte*, not *Idomeneo*), and especially Gluck, yet he was unable to utilize music in this drama to the extent of his hopes.

At a preliminary rehearsal the effect of the spoken chorus aroused much enthusiasm, but soon thereafter many of the choral passages had to be assigned to individual characters like Bohemund and Cajetan. Schiller planned to incorporate music into his drama and wrote Zelter about

> . . . a tragedy of mine, with the chorus of the old tragedies present, in which this effective voice was attempted on the old stage not without success . . . We do not consider it impossible to have the lyric intermezzos of the chorus, of which there are five or six, recited in song and accompanied by [instruments].

He hoped that Zelter would 'overwhelm us with a musical performance of it,'[24] but since Zelter was not in Weimar and no other composer in whom

Schiller had confidence was available, the history of
Die Braut von Messina is that of a spoken choral drama.
Shortly before writing Zelter about his drama,
Schiller told Iffland that 'the staging will not be
difficult, as the speeches of the chorus are not to be
accompanied with music,'[25] and this was the future
manner of performance of this drama during its
author's lifetime.

Buchwald states that some of Schiller's friends
thought that music in the style of Russian church
psalmody would have been highly suitable for the
choruses.[26] Had a composer been available whose
musical language was compatible with Schiller's
drama – Cherubini, Méhul, or Beethoven – the
history of *Die Braut von Messina* would have been
different, for the *Gesamtkunstwerk* would have been
a reality two generations before Wagner's music
dramas. Without music, *Die Braut von Messina* was
fated to remain one of the 'might-have-beens' of
musical and dramatic history.

Since 1785 Schiller had been interested in a drama
about the defense of Malta against the Turks by the
Knights of St. John. In even the preliminary
sketches for *Die Malteser* he specified a chorus consisting of sixteen knights. After finishing *Die Braut
von Messina* he expressed new interest in the drama
which he had laid aside, but the final sketches never
progressed beyond an annotated outline.

Since dramatic incidental music was purely functional, little care was taken to preserve it. Some music,
like Reichardt's music to *Macbeth*, circulated among

theatres, but it was usually more convenient for the Kapellmeister to write or arrange his own; thus during the first five years of *Wilhelm Tell's* existence there were settings not only by Destouches in Weimar but also by Bernhard Anselm Weber in Berlin and Gyrowetz in Vienna. Few examples of incidental music were published; a brief list of the music to Schiller's dramas in published examples consists of Zumsteeg's songs to *Die Räuber*, piano reductions of excerpts from Weber's settings of *Die Jungfrau von Orleans* and *Wilhelm Tell*, and a few passages of Destouches' music for the latter drama. Frequently incidental music to a given drama that was worn out, outmoded, or simply disliked by a new Kapellmeister was put aside and then thrown away, and virtually all of what was not discarded was destroyed through theatre fires or the Allied bombings of German cities during the second World War.

Incidental music was often a pastiche of the music of many composers. We have already seen Burney's description of a performance of Lessing's *Emilia Galotti* with music by three different composers, and Goethe described another frequent practice in *Wilhelm Meister*:

[The Baroness] sent for the musician who was at the head of the Count's private orchestra, partly so that he should compose the necessary pieces [for the play] and partly that he should choose suitable tunes from the stock of music.

For the second performance of *Die Räuber* Danzi's new entr'actes were used in addition to Zumsteeg's overture and songs, and three composers may have been involved in the music for *Wallensteins Lager*.

An equally lackadaisical attitude toward incidental music was displayed by the performers. In Mannheim the Kapellmeister chose or composed the incidental music but had nothing to do with the performance since his contract did not require him to direct the music for the theatrical productions. Spohr was pleased with his contract at the Theater an der Wien in Vienna in 1813 because he would be exempt from conducting or playing in performances of incidental music for plays. As a general rule the musicians detested having to play incidental music; they came to rehearsals and performances when they pleased, and one violinist even cut his finger in order to escape what he felt to be an onerous duty. Conductors would send their worst musicians to the stage director so that they would be used backstage or put in costume for onstage appearances and thus removed from the orchestra. In Rudolstadt the theatre musicians drank beer while on duty until forbidden to do so by the Prince in 1798. The position of musical director in a theatre was no sinecure; Eylenstein, who occupied this post in the minor theatres in the Duchy of Weimar during Goethe's time, had to serve as coach, timpanist, copyist, cembalist, and even as an actor in comedies.

The audiences for the dramas wanted to hear the incidental music played by a full orchestra, but seldom were Schiller's desires for effective music given an even adequate realization. The orchestra in Mannheim, after Karl Theodor moved his court to Munich in 1778, was no longer the 'army of generals' that thrilled Burney and Mozart; the orchestra in Dalberg's Nationaltheater, which played the music for the first performances of *Die Räuber* and *Fiesko*, consisted of only 27 players, some of whom were sons or pupils of the members of what was left of the court orchestra. The orchestra in Weimar was small, not very good, and had to be reinforced with Eberwein's ineffective *Stadtmusikanten*, who were chiefly used for music played on- or offstage. The orchestras were even smaller in the minor theatres in Lauchstädt or Erfurt. Even at the Königliche Nationaltheater in Berlin, where Schiller was able to hear the best music to his dramas, the orchestra contained only 25 players in 1801.

Schiller's desires for incidental music were better satisfied in Weimar than in Mannheim. Although *Die Räuber* and *Fiesko* contain much incidental music, none as such is specified in *Kabale und Liebe* and the indication for 'rustic music of flutes and oboes' in the opening scene of the prose version of *Don Carlos* was eliminated from the definitive verse version, in which the only music stipulated is Eboli's song. In 1786 Schiller wrote: 'In Mannheim I have, for reasons which would be too detailed, almost completely lost all interest in the theatre,' and Mirow believes that one of these reasons, as shown by the virtual elimination of incidental music from Schiller's last two early dramas, was the unfortunate musical situation at the Nationaltheater.[27] On the other hand, all of

Schiller's Weimar dramas except *Maria Stuart* are characterized by a lavish use of incidental music.

Schiller and Zumsteeg were lifelong friends, but Zumsteeg wrote incidental music for only *Die Räuber*. Schiller strove to get Zumsteeg's overture performed by praising it to Count Dalberg: 'I know it will be a masterpiece,' and in the foreword to the second edition of *Die Räuber* expressed the hope that the texts to the songs would be forgotten on account of Zumsteeg's music.[28] The overture and the incidental music have been lost; only the songs were published. The 19-year-old Franz Danzi wrote new entr'actes for subsequent performances of *Die Räuber* but these have also disappeared.

Mirow's statement that Ferdinand Fränzl wrote the music for the first performances of *Fiesko* is improbable since the composer was 13 years old at the time; Ignaz Fränzl is the most likely composer since he had also written music for Shakespeare's plays. Schiller mentions both Fränzls in his letters but not in connection with any dramatic music. Nothing is known about incidental music for *Kabale und Liebe* or *Don Carlos*, since what music is specified in these dramas can be freely inserted and need not have been specially composed.

Considerable doubt exists concerning the authorship of all of the music for the *Wallenstein* trilogy. The extent of the contributions of Kranz and Destouches has been disputed, and in any case the music has been lost.* Yet the most famous and popular example of incidental music to any of Schiller's dramas is the 'Reiterlied' by an amateur composer, Christian Jacob Zahn. Schiller hoped that Zelter would write its music 'because it will be sung in our German theatres and so many musical bunglers would be delighted to compose it,' but Zelter asked for further information about it and finally declined because 'it is nearly impossible to become familiar with a drama at second hand.' Schiller then turned to Körner but was dissatisfied with his setting:

> You must play the 'Reiterlied' lower than it is set, as you will see. It is a strange thing for a musician to have the cuirassier sing in a register that few female voices can reach. Otherwise the melody has pleased me . . . In the copy you sent me the melodies to the strophes are a little confused, and the players and singers would be bewildered in searching for them.[30]

A setting of the 'Reiterlied' which reached Schiller bore merely the initial Z as signature. Schiller thought that Zumsteeg had written this, but he denied it and stated that Zahn, whom Schiller had known as early as 1794, was the composer. He was delighted with Zahn's setting, remarking that 'this melody pleases me greatly and has deeply moved me

---

* Loewenberg (*Grove*, II, 677) attributes the incidental music to Kranz whereas Schaal (MGG, III, cols. 246-47) ascribes it to Destou ches.

as well as all those who have heard it sung in my presence,' and 'as often as I hear his melody . . . it gives me pleasure.'[31]

If Kranz did write any of the music for the *Wallenstein* trilogy, this was the extent of his composing music for Schiller's dramas. Kranz' life in Weimar was difficult because he fell into disfavor with Eberwein, Karoline Jagemann, and finally Goethe before leaving in 1803, and Schiller seems virtually to have ignored him after 1787.

On the other hand, Schiller seems to have placed more confidence in Destouches' musical ability. He thought the march for *Turandot* which Destouches played for him had a 'very good effect' and planned at least to have the composer examine Weber's music for the Berlin production of *Wilhelm Tell* 'to see what is in it.'[32] Destouches, we know, did write music for *Die Jungfrau von Orleans*, *Die Braut von Messina*, and *Wilhelm Tell*, and may have possibly composed at least some of the music for the *Wallenstein* trilogy. All of Destouches' music was thought lost when the Weimar court theatre burned in 1819, but the score of his music to *Wilhelm Tell* was discovered in 1955 and was used for performances of this drama to commemorate the sesquicentennial of Schiller's death.

The composition is scored for flutes, oboes, clarinets, and bassoons in pairs and strings, with no trumpets or timpani, although these instruments could be added and would be appropriate in the music to be played after the fall of the curtain in Act II. In the first act three horns and herdbells are to be used onstage, and the offstage wind band for the wedding march of Act IV consists of oboe, clarinet, bassoon, violas, and two horns. The overture is sectional, thematically and formally weak, and leads directly into 'Es lächelt der See,' the song opening the first act, in which the horns and herdbells are used. An unidentified entr'acte resembles a polka. The pastorale for Act IV consists merely of two groups of four measures with repeat marks, no doubt to be played as long as necessary. The wedding march in 6/8 in Act IV fulfills Schiller's requirement for 'sprightly music' but does not seem effective as music for any kind of procession. No setting of 'Mit dem Pfeil, dem Bogen' was included. Throughout the composition poverty of invention is distressingly evident, especially when compared with Bernhard Anselm Weber's music for this drama. Small wonder that Schiller sought other composers for his songs and dramatic music!

Weber had been musical director of the Königstadt theatre in Berlin since 1792. His settings of the incidental music to Schiller's plays have been the most viable and were used throughout the nineteenth century; his 'Mit dem Pfeil, dem Bogen' is still popular.

Schiller initially wanted Zelter to write the music for the Berlin production of *Wilhelm Tell*. 'I have different songs,' he wrote, 'which I would prefer to have composed by no one but you,' but explained that he did not know the 'theatre relationships' in Berlin and whether Zelter's participation would be an encroachment on the rights of the composers

attached to the theatres. Zelter evidently declined,
for Schiller subsequently wrote Iffland that he was
going to ask Weber about his settings of the song
and requested Iffland's help.[33]

When Schiller went to Berlin and saw a performance of *Die Jungfrau von Orleans* there he may have
met Weber, but was certainly able to hear his music
for the drama. Schiller's only known comment
about it was that the coronation march was too
long,[34] but the stage director was probably to blame
for this.

The accompaniment for Johanna's melodrama in
Act IV is the only other portion of Weber's music
for *Die Jungfrau von Orleans* to have survived, and
only in a piano reduction, for the score and parts
have been lost. Although Schiller specified 'flutes
and oboes behind the scene,' Weber scored the
accompaniment for two clarinets, two bassoons, and
two horns. The tempo throughout is poco adagio,
4/4 meter. The first section of 33 measures accompanies the first four stanzas of text; Weber indicates
that the conductor is to wait until the actress has
spoken all these lines before proceeding. Schiller's
directions that 'the music behind the scene changes
into a gentle, melting melody' are followed in the
next section; the final measure is to be governed by
the declamation so that it ends with the words
'Schmelzen sie in Wehmuts-Tränen.' Six measures
of fermata chords accompany the more animated
declamation which follows the instruction 'After a
pause, livelier.' Except for the telling phrase 'Ist
Mitleid Sünde?' there are two lines of text per

chord; one chord is sufficient to underscore the literary 'theme' of this passage. The final section, 23 measures long, coincides with the stage direction 'The flutes repeat, she sinks into a quiet melancholy.'

Weber's music to *Wilhelm Tell* is functional but very effective. His conscientiousness in writing suitable music for this drama is evident in his letter to Schiller about his attempt to find a suitable 'ranz des vaches' for the beginning of the overture and in his description of the overture he was planning to compose:

> The overture, according to my feeling and with what you yourself have expressed . . . can begin with a pastoral melody or ranz des vaches. Following this is the preparation of a grand tragic action. It is the sorrow of oppression, and the feeling of upward-striving freedom. Noise of battle and a splendid conclusion to the overture, which is gradually moving to the first pastoral melody. The curtain goes up, the melody continues, the fisherboy sings.[35]

The overture is scored for large orchestra but without trombones and 'Turkish music.' The introduction (pastorale larghetto, C major, 6/8) is characterized by melodies in the woodwinds and horns with sustained chords in the low strings at the ends of phrases. The merry first theme of the allegro moves into the minor mode during the transition (sorrow of oppression?) to the pleasant and lyrical second theme-group. A development section in which both themes are worked over leads to a short recapitulation. The coda, più presto, is justified by musical rather than dramatic reasons and is contradictory with Weber's letter to Schiller. A footnote at the conclusion of the overture indicates that its last 36 measures are to be used for the finale of Act II where Schiller's directions state: 'The orchestra joins in with a splendid spirited melody.' Evidently Weber changed the ending of the overture, for a contemporaneous reviewer, who compared the overture favorably with Gluck's instrumental compositions, mentioned that the coda 'returns to the mood of the beginning to lead into the first act.'[36]

The song "Es lächelt der See" opens the first act. Schiller stated that the second and third stanzas should be variations of the melody of the first stanza, evidently not variations in the musical sense but that the song should be through-composed rather than strophic. At the end of the first stanza an offstage horn solo leads to the shepherd's strophe, a three-part song in G minor with a middle section in tonic major. A fanfare leads to the chamois-hunter's strophe which is accompanied by two horns. Walther's song 'Mit dem Pfeil, dem Bogen' is accompanied solely by two horns in E-flat.

The cue in the score for the wedding march in Act IV is the conclusion of Tell's soliloquy. The march, sprightly and gay almost to the point of triviality, is scored for an offstage wind band of flute, two clarinets in C, two horns in C, trumpet in C, and two bassoons. The chorus of Barmherzige Brüder at the conclusion of this act is to consist of 20 to 24 male singers accompanied by four bassoons; the solemnity of this chorus is emphasized by the moderate tempo, the 4/2 time signature, the key of B-flat minor, and the a cappella writing in the middle section. Another march, scored like the wedding march, is to be played during the change of scene between the second and final scenes of the last act. No finale was written, for the coda of the overture could meet the requirements for 'while the music comes in again in a rapid tempo, the curtain falls.'

The settings of the incidental music to Schiller's dramas contain an amazing amount of music which has sunk into complete oblivion. The music by the composers of note deserves brief mention: Sigismund Neukomm, Sechter, and Ferdinand Ries wrote music for *Die Braut von Messina*, Lachner and Carl Maria von Weber for *Turandot*, and Ignaz von Seyfried, Moscheles, and Bruch for *Die Jungfrau von Orleans*. Schumann's overture to *Die Braut von Messina* is primarily a concert overture, and Wagner's overture to this drama is among his unpublished juvenilia. Smetana's *Valdštýnův Tábor* can be performed as a symphonic poem or, with a cut marked by the composer, as an overture to *Wallensteins Lager*. Schiller's *Macbeth* was one of several competing versions and had no special music composed for it; Reichardt's music was for Bürger's version and could be used only for melodramatic effects in Schiller's translation, and Spohr's *Macbeth* music was composed for Spiker's version. On the other hand, Borcherdt states that the reason why Schiller's dramatically more effective version of *Egmont* has not supplanted Goethe's original drama in the theatrical repertoire is that Beethoven's music cannot be used for this revision.[37]

In using music in producing Schiller's dramas, we must remember that most of the original music has vanished, and only Weber's music and Zahn's 'Reiterlied' possess intrinsic merit apart from their functional purpose. Although Schiller's dramas are not dated 'period pieces' like the plays of Iffland or Kotzebue, the idiom of contemporary music would still be quite discordant. Though Schiller did intensive research for his historical dramas, he was not above changing historical incidents to secure an increased effect (as witness the ending of *Die Jungfrau von Orleans!*); neither should the musical director strain for historical accuracy by using Burgundian chansons in *Die Jungfrau von Orleans* or setting 'Der Eichwald brauset' in the style of a continuo aria by Selle or Hammerschmidt. The music of Schiller's time or for forty years thereafter is the most appropriate for his dramas. Lesser-known overtures or symphonic first movements by Haydn (in his 'Sturm und Drang' style), Spohr, or Schumann; orchestrations of the Opus 45 marches by Beethoven or operatic marches by Méhul or Catel; and codas from unfamiliar pre- or early Romantic symphonies would be very effective. Since little attention was paid to stylistic unity by having one composer set all the incidental music, an interesting assortment could be compiled. The songs might have to be set anew since most of the settings of the poems in the dramas by Reichardt, Zumsteeg, or Schubert are too independently musical and would disturb the mood of the drama; some of Reichardt's settings are like the operatic *scena ed aria* with piano accompaniment. The use of familiar music like a well-known Beethoven overture to precede the play should be avoided because of the associations it would arouse in the minds of the audience.

III. MUSIC AS A LITERARY EFFECT

In contrast with Schiller's dramatic use of music to
intensify an action or to create an atmosphere, his
literary use of this medium serves to depict traits of
character or to heighten expression through metaphor. In addition, so much has been written about
the 'musical speech' of eighteenth-century German
lyric poetry that an attempt should be made to define
and clarify this expression.

A feeling for music is characteristic of many of
Schiller's major dramatic personages. In *Die Räuber*
both Karl and Franz Moor are amateur musicians,
and Amalia not only sings but also plays the guitar
and lute. In the middle of the song 'Hektors Abschied' (II, 2) Amalia inserts the comment 'Karl und
ich haben's oft zusammen zu der Laute gesungen,'
and in the reprise of this song (IV, 4) Karl and Amalia
sing to the accompaniment of a lute. In the following scene, after Karl has returned to his robber band,
he shows his depression by asking for his lute: 'ich
muss mich zurück lullen in meine Kraft . . .' and
singing the 'Römergesang.' Knudsen has advanced
the theory that the villainous Franz is not really a
musician and that his telling Amalia how he played
the clavier 'wenn alles um mich begraben lag in
Schatten und Schlummer' is merely an attempt to
impress her.[1]
Kraft, in his informative study of the historical
background of *Die Räuber*, has shown that the bandit
gangs of Thuringia frequently contained musicians;
'Krummfinger Baltzer's' robbers included instru-
mentalists and itinerant ballad singers of whom the

evil Spiegelberg, with his mention of a 'Bänkelsän-gerlied' (I, 2), his frequent references to music, and his Morität 'Geh' ich vorbey' (II, 3), is an example. Kraft conjectures that Spiegelberg and the other robbers are the elite of Baltzer's highwaymen.[2]

Fiesko contains many striking musical metaphors and much incidental music but only one musical character, the villainess Julia. In the ninth scene of Act III she works off her wrath by going 'angrily to a harpsichord' and playing an allegro, for which a 'Sturm und Drang' sonata movement by C. P. E. Bach would be appropriate. At the end of the scene her brother asks: 'Nun, Schwester? hast du deinen Zorn bald verklimpert?'

Schiller's most musical character is Miller in *Kabale und Liebe*. In the *dramatis personae* he is called a 'Stadtmusikant' or 'Kunstpfeifer,' virtually synonymous terms. Stadtmusikanten played for weddings, dances, church services, and reinforced court and theatre orchestras, but were citizens of the town, could accept pupils, were paid for performing at private functions, and were privileged over foreign musicians, tavern fiddlers, military bandsmen, and students.[3] As the curtain rises on the first act, Miller is putting his cello aside after practicing. Although his major instrument is the violin (I, 1; II, 4; III, 3) he is able to give lessons on the flute (II, 6; v, 3), and his reference to playing the lute (v, 1) may not be merely metaphorical. Miller is, therefore, a musical jack-of-all-trades, and that such musicians were common in eighteenth-century Germany is shown in Zelter's description of a Stadtmusikus:

If at first I considered George a rough, common
man, I soon learned to know him as a thoroughly
skilled musician. He played all of the current
instruments well, preferably cello and clarinet,
but he was unique as a player of the double bass.[4]

Miller is rough, coarse, blunt, and even scatological.
He has no opinions on music and his statements
about the art are extremely practical: 'Ich heisse
Miller, wenn Sie ein Adagio hören wollen' (II, 6).
To him music is a trade like plumbing or carpenter-
ing, not a means of aesthetic satisfaction or emotional release. When Ferdinand gives Miller a sum of
money, the musician replies:

Und auf dem Markt will ich meine Musikstunden
geben und Numero fünfe Dreikönig rauchen, und
wenn ich wieder auf den Dreibatzenplatz sitze,
soll mich der Teufel holen (V, 5).

Such statements have aroused the ire of those critics
with a Romantic over-idealization of music and
musicians; since the premiere of *Kabale und Liebe*
Miller has been attacked as a disgusting, boorish, and
commonplace character.

Ferdinand and Luise, the two lovers, represent on
the other hand the amateur musicians who were so
prevalent in the eighteenth century. Ferdinand met
Luise when he took flute lessons from Miller to find
'*Ruhe* für meine einsame Stunden' and later summa-
rizes the story of his star-crossed romance: 'Mann!
ich bezahle dir dein bisschen Flöte zu teuer ...

Unglückseliges Flötenspiel, das mir nie hätte ein-
fallen sollen' (v, 3). Luise plays the piano and invites
Ferdinand to 'accompany' her on the flute (v, 7), a
reference to the 'accompanied clavier' music of the
later eighteenth century. Lady Milford in this drama
is also musical; the study of 'ein wenig Filet und den
Flügel' (ii, 3) was part of her education as a gentle-
woman, and at the opening of Act ii she improvises
at the harpsichord to calm her agitation.

Whereas the musicians in the Thuringian robber
bands may have influenced the musical characterizations in *Die Räuber*, the musical portraits in the
Sturm und Drang dramas may have affected Schiller's musical depictions in his other prose dramas.
Lenz' musicians are mostly professionals, but Rehaar
in *Der Hofmeister* differs from Miller in that Rehaar
is almost childlike in his absorbtion in his art and is
a figure of scorn through his cowardly subservience,
and Schlankard in the unfinished *Der tugendhafte
Taugenichts* is perhaps the first appearance of the
emotional, sentimental, romantic musician as a
literary figure. Klinger frequently depicted amateur
musicians (especially clavier players) in his dramas,
and the effect of Karoline's clavier playing in *Sturm
und Drang* is much like that of Streicher's on young
Schiller. Furthermore, in the preceding chapter we
have encountered many amateur musicians as
members of Schiller's circle.

Biondello in *Der Geisterseher* is an example of the
servant-musician who was a fixture in many eighteenth-century households. His master, the Prince,
discovered him 'varying a touching adagio with

some fine improvised variations' and wanted to
discharge him because he was too good a musician
to be a mere servant, but Biondello refused this offer
and gladly accepted the duty of playing the Prince to
sleep with tender music and awakening him with
lively pieces. Biondello's talent and the Prince's
appreciation of it highlight the loyalty of the one
and the romantic character of the other.

An enthusiasm for music leads to Don Carlos'
downfall. When he hears Princess Eboli playing and
singing in order to establish an atmosphere con-
ducive to romance, the effect compels him to exclaim:

> Und Laute – das weiss Gott im Himmel – Laute
> Die lieb' ich bis zur Raserei. Ich bin
> Ganz Ohr, ich weiss nichts von mir selber, stürze
> Ins Kabinett, der süssen Künstlerin,
> Die mich so himmlisch rührte, mich so mächtig
> Bezauberte, ins schöne Aug' zu sehen (II, 8).

The scene in *Wallensteins Tod* (III, 4) where the
dispirited Wallenstein asks his daughter Thekla to
sing for him is one of Schiller's strongest musical
characterizations:

> Komm her, mein Mädchen. Setz dich zu mir.
> Es ist ein guter Geist auf deinen Lippen.
> Die Mutter hat mir deine Fertigkeit
> Gepriesen, es soll eine zarte Stimme
> Des Wohllauts in dir wohnen, die die Seele
> Bezaubert. Eine solche Stimme brauch'
> Ich jetzt, den bösen Dämon zu vertreiben,
> Der um mein Haupt die schwarzen Flügel schlägt.

But despite the additional urgings of her stepmother and aunt, Thekla is so distraught that she refuses to perform. In the more dramatically effective stage versions the orchestra starts a ritornello for a song, but when she is to begin singing, she throws her zither aside and rushes from the room.

When Attinghausen in *Wilhelm Tell* tries to dissuade Rudenz from entering the Austrian service and thus leaving his Swiss homeland, Schiller has him refer to the legend that the 'ranz des vaches' made Swiss soldiers homesick (II, I), but Goethe, who had visited Switzerland, questioned the validity of this passage: as far as he knew the 'ranz des vaches' was not played outside of Switzerland and the soldiers were affected by *not* hearing this melody.[5]

Schiller's musical metaphors are either concrete or indefinite. Concrete metaphors consist of definite musical objects or activities, whereas indefinite metaphors rely on the use of musical terms in an ambiguous sense in order to create an atmosphere or establish non-musical shades of meaning. Thus the mention of a musical term may, depending on its context, be crassly literal, gloriously poetic, or even ironically sardonic. Although instruments, or the act of playing or singing, are used to characterize personages in the drama, frequently certain instruments are also used in a metaphorical sense.

'Posaune' is not a trombone, but an obsolete instrument which helps create the atmosphere of the Middle Ages ('Der Graf von Habsburg') or as Luther used it in I Corinthians 15, 51-52; for example in *Die Räuber* (v, 1) 'da erscholl's wie aus ehernen Posaunen: Erde, gib deine Toten ...' or, more poetically and less dramatically, 'des Gerüchtes donnernde Posaune' in *Don Carlos* (ii, 2); it can also mean an emphatic declaration, as in *Fiesko* (ii, 9): 'ich posaune jetzt deinen Meuchelmord aus.'

Although 'Horn' is occasionally a "Füllhorn" or the horns of an animal, it generally occurs in a musical context. The horn summons herds ('Der Alpenjäger') or announces glad tidings ('Graf Eberhard der Greiner') but is most often a signalling instrument. In using the horn to create the imagery of the hunt, Schiller contrasts the feminine and masculine views of this sport. *Maria Stuart* contains a beautiful example of this poetic imagery, where the horn awakens not only Maria's love of the hunt but also her regrets at no longer being able to participate in it and her homesickness (iii, 1):

> Hörst du das Hifthorn? Hörst du's klingen,
> Mächtigen Rufes, durch Feld und Hain?
> Auch, auf das mutige Ross mich zu schwingen,
> An den fröhlichen Zug mich zu reihn!
> Noch mehr! O die bekannte Stimme
> Schmerzlich süsser Erinnerung voll.
> Oft vernahm sie mein Ohr mit Freuden,
> Auf des Hochlands bergigten Heiden,
> Wenn die tobende Jagd erscholl.

Whereas a masculine view of the hunt – joy in the chase and enthusiasm aroused by the hunting horns – is expressed by a member of Don Manuel's retinue in *Die Braut von Messina*:

Denn die Jagd ist ein Gleichnis der Schlachten,
Des ernsten Kriegsgotts lustige Braut –
Man ist auf mit dem Morgenstrahl,
Wenn die schmetternden Hörner laden
Lustig hinaus in das dampfende Tal . . .

Trumpets, integral parts of martial scenes, are used
not only literally but also metaphorically, as in *Die
Piccolomini* (i, 4). The drum, however, is Schiller's
military instrument par excellence and is closely associated with warlike metaphors. The drum calls
soldiers together literally (*Die Jungfrau von Orleans*,
v, 8) or metaphorically (*Die Piccolomini*, ii, 7;
Wallensteins Tod, iii, 13), and in the false account of
Karl's death 'zog ihn der Hall von Friedrich's sieg-
reicher Trommel' during the Seven Years' War
(*Die Räuber*, ii, 2). The first cuirassier in *Wallensteins
Lager* uses 'Trommel' in a slang sense ('Aber nicht
auf mir trommeln lassen') and Spiegelberg in *Die
Räuber* (i, 2) refers to this instrument ironically in
asking 'oder bei klingendem Spiel nach dem Takt
der Trommel spazieren gehn?' The timpani (Pauken) are not used as martial instruments, but 'ein
bacchantisches Getön/Von Reigen und von Pauken'
accompany a carouse in King Philip's palace (*Don
Carlos*, i, 4).

Schiller's most vivid metaphorical employment
of the drum occurs in *Kabale und Liebe* (ii, 2) when
Lady Milford's servant is describing the gathering of
the soldiers who have been sold to fight in America.
The 'shrilly piercing' drums gave the signal for the
separation of fathers from their families 'mitunter

das polternde Wirbelschlagen, damit der Allwissende uns nicht sollte beten hören.'

Frau Vischer and other friends probably influenced Schiller's frequent references to keyboard instruments. In *Kabale und Liebe* the piano (v, 7) and the harpsichord (II, 1, 3), also mentioned in *Fiesko* (III, 9), are specifically designated, but all the other references are simply to the clavier, which could mean either of these instruments or the clavichord. Loesser believes that the piano is the instrument described in 'Laura am Klavier' because of the 'violent contrasts' depicted in the music which is being played.[6] Schiller uses the clavier in some of his most striking metaphors, as in *Die Räuber* (v, 1), where Franz Moor disputes the immortality of the soul with Pastor Moser: 'Empfindung ist Schwingung einiger Saiten, und das zerschlagene Klavier tönet nicht mehr,' and in *Kabale und Liebe* (IV, 7) where Lady Milford describes Luise's falling in love for the first time: 'Auf dem unberührten Klavier der erste einweihende Silberton!'

Because of its musical setting, *Kabale und Liebe* contains most of the miscellaneous references to musical instruments. Miller has a derogatory view of his cello: 'eh' will ich mein Violonzello zerschlagen und Mist im Sonanzboden führen' (I, 1) and in the next scene threatens to throw it at his wife's head. His reference to the orchestra provoked Moritz' epithet of 'disgusting':[7]

FRAU: Du kannst dem Herzog rekommendiert worden sein. Er kann dich ins Orchester verlangen.

MILLER: . . . Orchester! Ja, wo du Kupplerin den Diskant wirst heulen und mein blauer Hinterer den Konterbass vorstellen! (II, 4).

Yet Schiller uses a striking orchestral metaphor in *Fiesko* when the hero describes the impending revolt: 'Zum schaudernden Konzert alle Instrumente gestimmt.' (II, 16).

The use of the violin as a stage prop shows an interesting contrast between Lenz and Schiller. In the former's *Die neue Menoza* Zierau plays the violin (V, 2) and later exhibits discouragement by throwing his instrument on the table. In *Kabale und Liebe* (III, 4) Ferdinand is so emotionally overwrought when he thinks Luise unfaithful to him that words fail him: he seizes a violin, attempts to play it, then rips off the strings, dashes the instrument to the ground, and stamps it to pieces.

Chiefly because of their association with antiquity, the plucked stringed instruments frequently occur as components of poetic metaphors. The zither occurs only in 'Pegasus im Joche,' and the lute is mentioned chiefly in the dramas: we have seen this instrument in the hands of Karl and Amalia in *Die Räuber*, and Maria was deprived of it by her jailers because she played 'verbuhlte Lieder' on it (*Maria Stuart*, I, I). In 'Der Triumph der Liebe' the lute conveys an alliterative sense of repose: 'Liebe, Liebe lispelt nur/ Auf die Laute der Natur.'

The harp occurs only in the poems, usually in a feminine sense. In 'Würde der Frauen' the sensitive soul of the woman is compared to an Aeolian harp gently shaken by zephyrs, whereas in 'Elysium' the dreaming pilgrim is 'eingesungen von Harfengezitter,' and the Maeonides play harps in 'Die Künstler.'

The lyre, in contrast, is generally a masculine but also a peaceful instrument, most strikingly portrayed in 'Die Kraniche des Ibykus,' when the hero is attacked by the murderers but cannot resist:

> Doch bald ermattet sinkt die Hand,
> Sie hat der Leier zarte Saiten,
> Doch nie des Bogens Kraft gespannt.

The lyre is an instrument of joy ('Die vier Weltalter') and its masculinity is emphasized in 'Männerwürde,' originally entitled 'Kastraten und Männer.' One of Schiller's principal theses in his philosophical poems was that the culture of his time had declined since the ideal days of Greece, and the lyre is used to express this idea poignantly in 'Die Sänger der Vorwelt':

> Ach, noch leben die Sänger, nur fehlen die Taten,
> die Lyra
> Freudig zu wecken, es fehlt, ach! ein empfangen-
> des Ohr.

'Saiten,' or its compounds like 'Saitenruf' and 'Saitenspiel,' is the most ambiguous of Schiller's

instrumental terms. Seldom is it used literally, as in
'Laura am Klavier.' In the poems 'Saiten' is associated with the atmosphere of antiquity, but in the
dramas this word is divorced from any direct association with mythology and perhaps thus pro-
duces a telling effect in metaphors. One powerful
example occurs in *Don Carlos* (IV, 21) a drama in
which similar metaphors occur (*e.g.*, III, 10; V, 4):

> Gehört die süsse Harmonie, die in
> Dem Saitenspiele schlummert, seinem Käufer,
> Der es mit taubem Ohr bewacht? Er hat
> Das Recht erkauft, in Trümmern es zu schlagen,
> Doch nicht die Kunst, dem Silberton zu rufen
> Und in des Liedes Wonne zu zerschmelzen.

'Spiel,' occurring almost exclusively as a noun, is
most often present in compounds, especially
'Saitenspiel' and very tellingly in the 'eiserne Würfel-
spiel' of 'Die Schlacht,' but is sometimes used
separately, even to describe vocal music, for example
'Der Stimme seelenvolles Spiel/Entfaltete sich zum
Gesange' in 'Die Künstler.'

Vocal metaphors are more frequent than instrumental metaphors in Schiller's works; although
fewer vocal terms occur, they are used more often.
Some ambiguity, moreover, is characteristic of many
of the vocal metaphors, either through anthropo-
morphic attribution of human acts to animals, such
as the singing of birds, or through a mixing of
metaphors in having 'Gesang' refer to instruments.

Though Schiller sometimes uses 'Gesang' and 'Lied' interchangably as a collective noun meaning song, he usually distinguishes between 'Gesang' as the general category of vocal music and 'Lied' as specific songs, as in 'Die Kraniche des Ibykus':

> . . . Ibykus, der Götterfreund.
> Ihm schenkte des Gesanges Gabe,
> Der Lieder süssen Mund Apoll.

Another comparison between the two words can be drawn from two examples with the same theme, song as the preserver of tradition. Schiller uses 'Gesang' to create the idea of antiquity in 'Die Götter Griechenlands':

> Was unsterblich im Gesang soll leben,
> Muss im Leben untergehn.

Whereas he uses 'Lied' to refer to what may have been traditions almost as remote but in a context where a more realistic atmosphere is demanded (*Wilhelm Tell*, II, 2):

> So ist es wahr, wie's in den Liedern lautet
> Dass wir von fernher in das Land gewallt?

'Gesang,' however, is customarily used in a general and atmospheric sense. A beautiful atmospheric use of this word occurs in Charles VII's description of southern France (*Die Jungfrau von Orleans*, I, 7): '. . . da wohnen die Gesänge,/Und schöner blüht das

Leben und die Liebe,' whereas its absence is part of the frightening description of the Fates in *Die Braut von Messina*:

Drunten aber in Tiefen sitzen
Lichtlos, ohne Gesang und Sprache
Der Themis Töchter, die nie vergessen.

Schiller always uses the term 'Lied' to convey a mood of irony, as in Franz' soliloquy in *Die Räuber* (IV, 2), or when Wallenstein learns of Octavio Piccolomini's betrayal (*Wallensteins Tod*, III, 7), he remarks: 'Das alte Lied! Einmal, für allemal,/Nichts mehr von diesem törigten Verdacht!'

That song is power is the thesis of 'Die Macht des Gesanges,' where song is compared with thunder and a stream of rain from cliffs, yet can also draw fugitives back to the customs of their homelands. The individual singer is equally powerful: in 'Der Graf von Habsburg' he is the

> ... Bringer der Lust,
> Der mit süssem Klang mir bewege die Brust
> Und mit göttlich erhabenen Lehren.

Needless to say, Schiller was not referring to the opera singers of the time but to the bards of antiquity and the Middle Ages.

A reverence for such singers indicates the impractical character of Charles VII in *Die Jungfrau von Orleans*. In the opening scene of the first act Dunois complains to Du Chatel that the King is not inter-

ested in leading his army against the English but
prefers to remain at court, surrounded by 'Gaukel-
spieler und Troubadours.' In the next scene, when
a group of minstrels appears before the King and Du
Chatel informs him that they cannot be paid because
the treasury is empty, Charles replies:

> Edle Sänger dürfen
> Nicht ungeehrt von meinem Hofe ziehn.
> Sie machen uns den dürren Zepter blühn,
> Sie flechten den unsterblich grünen Zweig
> Des Lebens in die unfruchtbare Krone,
> Sie stellen herrschend sich den Herrschern gleich,
> Aus leichten Wünschen bauen sie sich Throne,
> Und nicht im Raume liegt ihr harmlos Reich:
> Drum soll der Sänger mit dem König gehen,
> Sie beide wohnen auf der Menschheit Höhen!

Schiller rarely uses the word 'Stimme' to mean the
singing voice; usually it occurs in an anthropo-
morphic sense, as where such disparate objects as
the cranes in 'Die Kraniche des Ibykus' or the bell
in 'Das Lied von der Glocke' have a metaphorical
vocal apparatus. In 'Kassandra' he makes a sharp
contrast between the prophetic and the singing voice
when the protagonist remarks:

> Nimmer sang ich freud'ge Lieder
> Seit ich d e i n e Stimme bin.

'Chor' seldom means a church choir, as in 'Der Gang
nach dem Eisenhammer,' but indicates a group: the

'Chor der Engel' in 'An die Freude' and *Die Jungfrau von Orleans* (v, 14) and 'der Götter sel'gem Chor' in 'Das Eleusische Fest.' 'Die Künstler' is especially rich in choral references – 'Eumenidenchor,' 'Der Sorgen schauervoller Chor,' and 'Kämonen Chor' are examples.

'Ton' has many meanings for Schiller, but he sometimes employed it in a musically metaphorical sense, as in his description of peace in *Die Braut von Messina*:

> Süsses Tönen entlockt er der Flöte,
> Und das Echo des Berges wird wach.

or quite literally in 'Laura am Klavier': 'Zauberin! Mit Tönen, wie/Mich mit Blicken, zwingst du sie.' In 'Kassandra' and *Die Braut von Messina* 'Ton' refers to funeral music. On the other hand, 'Melodie' usually describes the song of birds.

Aside from 'Lied,' 'Hymnus' is the musical category which Schiller mentions most frequently in a poetic sense. His usage derives from Sulzer's definition of the word as '[a song] of praise to the gods,' which is also Herder's understanding of the term.[8] The Erinnyes have a 'Hymnus' in 'Die Kraniche des Ibykus,' 'Jubelhymnen' occur in 'Kassandra,' and 'Eine Hymne' is the subtitle of 'Der Triumph der Liebe.' Schiller's mixture of Deism, Christianity, and Grecian allegorical elements in 'An die Freude' is shown in the phrase 'Seraphs Hymnus.' Of the other musical categories, 'madrigal' in *Maria Stuart* (II, 1) is used in its poetic rather than musical sense, and Schiller's references to opera in *Kabale und Liebe* and 'Die schlimmen Monarchen' are best discussed in the context of his musical aesthetics.

'Harmonie' is one of Schiller's favorite philosophical terms, but its employment is no more limited to music than is the English word 'harmony.' Schiller's use of this term in a musical sense is an ingredient of his most telling metaphors, one of the most effective of these being the taking of a single note from a chord, expressed poetically in 'Das verschleierte Bild zu Sais:'

> Nimm einen Ton aus einer Harmonie,
> Nimm eine Farbe aus dem Regenbogen –
> Und alles, was dir bleibt, ist nichts, so lang'
> Das schöne All der Töne fehlt und Farben . . .

or prosaically in *Kabale und Liebe* (1, 4): 'Wer kann den Bund zwoer Herzen lösen oder die Töne eines Akkords auseinander reissen?'

'Harmonie' is a synonym for music itself (the 'Saitenharmonie' of the Muses in 'Der Triumph der Liebe'), or is associated with the gods of Greece, as 'Des Olympus Harmonien' in 'Das Ideal und das Leben,' or with Nature. 'Die Künstler' abounds in ambiguous uses of 'Harmonie:' 'Harmonienbach,' 'Sein Geist zerrinnt in Harmonienmeere,' 'Harmonienspiele,' and the like, but 'harmon'schen Band' is a reference not to music but to Nature. 'Leiht er den Sphären seine Harmonie' resembles the allusions, based on Ptolemaic astronomy, to the 'music of the spheres.' One of Schiller's finest musical metaphors occurs in this poem:

Schon sieht man Schöpfungen aus Schöpfungen erstehen,
  Aus Harmonien Harmonie.

He previously expressed this idea in stating that one of the poet's tasks was to '[bereiten] uns von der Harmonie des Kleinen auf die Harmonie des Grossen.'[9] The ending of 'Die Künstler' (ll. 458-473) has been viewed as an oscillation between truth and 'Harmonie,' with the latter word synonymous with beauty.[10]

Although for Herder, influenced by music, 'Harmonie' was 'agreeable, delightful, and often enchanting,'[11] for Schiller this word as a poetic-philosophical term derived chiefly from his readings in mythology and Greek philosophy. Harmony, in the Grecian sense, had a variety of meanings, ranging from 'fitting together' or 'the existence of two or more distinguishing entities somehow capable of mutual adjustment' to 'the motion of the heavens, the cycle of the seasons, and the idea of primary physical materials or elements.' Music as 'harmony' came between these two different levels of meaning, but in the sense that the intrinsically musical nature could be united with the idea of abstract generality.[12]

Schiller makes few (and those few, contradictory) references to music itself. He enthusiastically praises it in 'Laura am Klavier' ('Ist's die Sprache, lüg mir nicht/Die man in Elysen spricht?') and overstates it in *Die Jungfrau von Orleans;* but on the other hand

he refers to it ironically in *Die Räuber*: 'Hochzeit-
musik' as the burning of the castle (v, 2), and 'Eine
Nachtmusik, davon einem die Zähn' klappern und
die Nägel blau werden' (iv, 5) as the shrieking of the
owls around old Moor's prison.

Schiller's musical metaphors have several features
in common. As many of the previously cited examples show, many of these metaphors tend to come in
clusters, often around a key word like 'Saiten,'
'Harmonie,' or 'Gesang.' The male characters in the
dramas refer to music more frequently than do the
women, and the women who say the most about
music are Schiller's least feminine characters, Amalia
and Johanna. The men who utter musical metaphors
are either the romantic young men like the Moor
brothers, Ferdinand, Don Carlos, and Charles vii,
or are the hardened characters like Spiegelberg or
Wallenstein whose mention of music is chiefly
ironic. Knudsen has remarked that Schiller's later
musical metaphors are better than his earlier ones;[13]
this is true not only of his poems but also of his
dramas, where the musical metaphors in the later
plays are less frequent than in the earlier ones but
are more effective.

That German lyric poetry of the eighteenth century
was written in a 'musical' poetic language is a
commonly repeated statement made by students of
this period. For example, Burdach says that the
secret of German poetry, beginning with Klopstock,
is 'latent music;' Fricke, that the poetry of the
Göttinger Hain 'transports the soul irresistibly

through music'; and Dilthey, that the poems by 'the great lyrical, musical genius' Klopstock contain 'proud and exalted melodies.'[14]

A partial explanation of the idea of 'musical speech' was the theory held by many eighteenth-century writers on literature that poetry and language had their origins in music. Although John Brown was not the first to advance this hypothesis, his writings influenced most subsequent German critics, especially Hamann and Herder. Whereas Brown was attacking the divorce of music from poetry with the resultant decline of both arts, Hamann asserted that 'Poetry is the mother tongue of the human race . . . song [is older] than declamation,' and Herder went so far as forcefully to declare in italics: 'The first speech of the human race was song.' He supported his statement with the argument that prayer was the origin of poesy: the accentuation, polymetric feet, and exalted tones of speaking made the prayer 'sung;' then came equal poetic feet; when these new texts were sung before the people to make a deeper impression on them, the poetic tone was elevated, and when accompanied by music these prayers became *'the first naturally rough compositions . . . the holy songs*, which have belonged to the first productions of poetry among all peoples.'[15] Only a few of the critics of the time resisted the trend to postulate a symbiosis between music and language: Lessing called Dryden's 'Ode on St. Cecilia's Day' a 'complete musical painting' but concluded that 'colors are not notes and ears are not eyes,' and Sulzer remarked:

> ... there is nothing easier to feel than the differ-
> ence between song and speech, but it is very
> difficult to describe it. Both are a succession of
> different tones which differ through high and low
> as well as through their special formation.[16]

Rhythm is the most important ingredient in a
'musical' poetry, with line-lengths, meter, and the
actual sounds of the words (including assonance and
alliteration) secondary considerations. The French
Alexandrines of the early eighteenth century were
musically limited because of their monotonous
iambic lockstep and end-rhymes, hence Klopstock
turned to a non-patterned meter in which the rhythm
would be determined by the sense, the content of
feeling in the single parts of the sentence, and the
musical definition of the foot, thus avoiding mechanical terminal rhymes with a constantly recurring
accent on the rhyme syllable. Two of the most
important examples of an epic musical speech –
Klopstock's *Der Messias* and Schiller's *Die Braut von
Messina* – are based on models which were originally
intimately connected with music, respectively the
Psalms and Greek drama. In lyric poetry of the time
recurring irregularities in line-length within individual stanzas provide interest when a basic metric
regularity and rhyme scheme are maintained; thus
among Schiller's immediate precursors Hagedorn
and Uz as well as Klopstock can be considered
'musical poets' whereas Gleim, despite his *Preussi-
sche Kriegslieder*, and von Kleist, whose *Cissides und
Paches* (although each individual canto is called

'Gesang') Knudsen considered to be an example of writing by one with no vocation for musical poetry, are 'unmusical' poets.[17]

To the eighteenth-century critic the ear was the final determiner of the 'musicality' of a given poem, whether it were declaimed aloud or set to music. In Herder's words, 'the ear is closest to the soul – just because it is an inner sensation;' the eye is a 'cold observer' but 'hearing alone is the most intimate, the deepest of the senses.'[18] Yet when Schiller called Klopstock a 'musical poet,' he was not thinking of prosody, rhythm, or line-lengths, but merely of mood:

> I say *musical*, to draw attention to the double relationship of poetry with music and with the pictorial arts. The more poetry either imitates a definite *object*, as the pictorial arts do, or the more it brings forth merely a definite state of mind, without having a definite object necessary, can it be called pictorial (plastic) or musical. The latter expression thus refers not merely to that which in poetry is actually (according to its material) music, but generally to all those effects which it is able to bring forth without dominating the power of imagination through a definite object, and in this sense I call Klopstock by preference a musical poet.[19]

He also insisted that the musical poet be able 'to put a text to any emotion' and at the same time be able to 'support any symbol of imagination and give it a

definite feeling.' Furthermore, he considered music
to be synonymous with inspiration: a 'certain musical condition of the soul' preceded his 'poetic idea'
and his 'clear definition of content,' of which he was
at times unsure in the course of his creative process.[20]

Practical musicians, when confronted with the
question of 'musical' poetry, tended to evade dis-
cussing this problem. Virtually every study of
Klopstock's poetry contains the anecdote about
J. A. P. Schulz, when he was asked to set one of
Klopstock's odes: 'Komponieren soll ich das? Das
ist ja schon Musik!' Zelter, a composer with a strong
interest in poetry, responded bluntly to Schiller's
inquiry concerning a 'musical' but unnamed poem:

> I consider it somewhat musical . . . You can well
> ask me what I mean by 'musical' and I will there-
> fore tell you at once that I don't rightly know,
> but that I know from other musicians that they
> also don't know, and that most of them are so
> ignorant as not to know they don't know . . . We
> musicians have no exact definition for what we
> call 'musical.'[21]

Among present-day scholars Silz is the principal
exponent of the idea that Schiller's poetic language
possesses musical characteristics: for instance, in the
opening scene of Act III of *Maria Stuart* he finds a
'virtually musical antiphony of voices and rhythms,'
which can be supported by Schiller's own statement
that in this scene 'the change in the rhythm causes a

peculiar musical effect;' Storz considers this scene to be virtually an operatic duet.[22]

Morgan has recently advanced the interesting hypothesis of 'musical pitch' in poetry: poetry is 'read' on levels of high, middle, or low speaking pitch or in a tessitura which might 'ride on a musically inclined plane, as it were, going either up or down.'[23] In attempting to repeat Morgan's experiment with Schiller's poems, I have found it almost impossible to isolate an abstract pitch-level in the poems with whose musical settings I was at the time familiar. The dialogued poems have an alternation of pitch levels, and the long poems, especially the philosophical ones with contrasting stanza or line lengths, do not lend themselves to this type of analysis. A close connection does exist between pitch and tempo: the faster the speed of declamation, the higher the tessitura. The following poems are suitable for a repetition of Morgan's experiments, but the reader is cautioned that such an evaluation is purely subjective.

Low pitch: Der Abend, Nadowessiers Totenlied, Die deutsche Muse, Hoffnung, Sprüche des Konfuzius.

Medium pitch: Würde der Frauen, Kassandra, Die Sänger der Vorwelt, Nänie, Laura am Klavier.

High pitch: Der Tanz, Der Jüngling am Bache, Pompeji und Herkulanum, Der Flüchtling, Die unüberwindliche Flotte.

Morgan's hypothesis could also be utilized as a guide to casting the singing characters in Schiller's dramas. In *Die Räuber*, Amalia would be a lyric

soprano, Karl a lyric tenor, and Spiegelberg a
gravelly baritone; Princess Eboli in *Don Carlos*
would be a lyric soprano (not a contralto as in
Verdi's opera); Thekla in *Die Piccolomini* would be a
mezzo-soprano; and a boy would portray Walther
in *Wilhelm Tell*.

To the logical positivist the question of musical
speech in poetry would be a synthetic proposition, a
probable hypothesis, and not 'meaningful.' The
arguments used in support of the theory of musical
speech are subjective and depend as much, if not
more, on the musical imagination of the critic as
of the poet. Attempts precisely to define musical
speech are characterized principally by contradiction
and uncertainty as well as by subjective views. What
critics have viewed as a musical language is not
identical with a poetic language suitable for musical
setting: for example, the only viable setting of
Klopstock's *Messias*, an epitome of musical speech
in eighteenth-century German poetry, is the choral
finale of Mahler's second symphony in which only
short and isolated fragments of this poem are used,
and we shall subsequently see the great difficulty
which Schiller's poetic language posed for composers. Finally, of all the factors which enter into
'musical speech' – assonance, alliteration, inversion,
telescoped or compound words, rhyme, meter,
stanzaic construction, line length, and rhythm –
only the last four seem to be genuine consituents of
such speech.

Schiller used a love for music as a means of portraying many of the personages in his dramas, and
in presenting these characters he makes numerous
references to music. A love for music is characteristic of such different individuals as Don Carlos and
Wallenstein, and references to this art are typical of
such contrasting figures as Luise and Spiegelberg.
Although the employment of musical metaphors
(which are present in the poems of Uz, Klopstock,
and even Gleim) is not unique with Schiller, he used
them effectively to create not only a poetic but also a
philosophical atmosphere. Schiller's 'musical speech'
is more evident to critics than it was to the poet, and
what he meant by the musical atmosphere of a poem
or in his own creative process was determined by
mood rather than by literary techniques.

Schiller also incorporated his love for and knowledge of music and its effects into his philosophical writings. In them he stated his formal views of the aesthetics of music, and in his letters and conversations his informal views on music, its genres, and its practitioners. Fully to understand the circumstances behind his views on music as an art, we must understand the circumstances which caused Schiller, who described himself as a 'pitiable layman' in musical matters during the period of his most important musical writings, to pronounce his judgments on this art.

During the first half of the eighteenth century German writings on music were practical works directed toward the professional musician or the skilled amateur; examples of these are the critical writings of Scheibe or the detailed descriptions of musical practice by Johann Mattheson. In the middle years of the century the ideas on music of Rousseau and the French Encyclopédistes, whose works were translated into German, aroused among German philosophers and critics an increasing concern with music in the establishment of aesthetic systems. Whereas Gottsched and Lessing were primarily interested in the practical considerations of dramatic music, and Klopstock and Gerstenberg were musically noteworthy solely because of their collaborations, respectively, with Gluck and C. P. E. Bach, both Herder and Kant have often been called the founders of German musical aesthetics, Schubart and Reichardt were professional musicians as well as journalists, Heinse had an excellent preparation in music, and Goethe's relationship to this art has brought into print a small library of books and monographs.

The great rise of interest in music among these literary figures can be explained by the threefold division of the musical world into professional, connoisseur, and appreciator (Künstler, Kenner, Liebhaber). The professional would seem to be the best judge of art but is not free from prejudice; on the other hand, the appreciator has a lively feeling for the effects which art creates, but his impressions are the results of emotions rather than systematic reasoning. The connoisseur occupies a position midway between the professional and the appreciator: in Sulzer's words a connoisseur 'is in a position to deliver an opinion on works of art according to their inner worth and to value the different degrees of their perfection.' He earns this reputation through 'long practice and experience of purified taste and insight into the nature and essence of art.' Kretzschmar draws an analogy between the philosopher of music (the connoisseur) and the physician who can diagnose and treat illnesses without having suffered personally from them, and Schering has made the best concise definition of the three groups: the appreciator takes pleasure in 'hearing or playing music,' the connoisseur 'takes the trouble to be able to judge music,' whereas the presence of technical facility and the absence of the critical faculty characterizes the professional.[1]

Schiller's musical pilgrimage, which we have traced in Chapter I, took him down the road from

amateur to connoisseur. Although he was not as
well grounded in the theory or history of this art
as were Herder and Heinse, he had more extensive
experience with it than Kant and more innate
sensitivity to it than Goethe. Above all, he was
willing to seek advice from those whose preparation
in music was greater than his.

In his philosophical writings before 1786 Schiller
was concerned chiefly with musical metaphors such
as occur in his early poems and which display the
technical knowledge of music which he acquired
from his friends at the Karlsschule. One of his most
apt analogies is the comparison of the sympathetic
vibration of strings with the stimulus an object gives
the nerves and the subsequent reaction by the brain,
or how 'the happy string in the body [affects] the
happy string in the soul ... the sad tone in the
former the sad tone in the latter.'[2] However, he only
seldom stated a philosophy of music: music is a part
of the rise of civilization, with art leading to science
and virtue, and the 20-year-old philosopher preferred the sound of stringed instruments to the
murmur of a brook and disliked the cawing of
ravens. 'What pleases me I call melodious and
beautiful; hateful and unmelodious, what vexes me,'[3]
is a remark typical of his early aesthetic theory.

Schiller did not display a strong interest in the
philosophic side of music until the opening of 1793,
when he wrote Körner:

I am doubtful of my views on music, for my ears
are already too old; still I am hardly eager that my

theory of beauty would run aground on music.
Perhaps there is some musical material which you
can use.

Körner recommended that he read Rousseau's
Dictionnaire de Musique, especially 'the articles which
do not pertain to the details of this art,' and Burney's
General History of Music for information about the
music of antiquity. Schiller subsequently replied
that he had read Sulzer's *Allgemeine Theorie der
schönen Künste* and a book by 'Kirschberger,' without
doubt Kirnberger's *Die Kunst des reinen Satzes in der
Musik*. After thoroughly investigating the records
of the libraries in Weimar and Erfurt (no records
of book circulation were kept at the time in Jena),
Knudsen concluded that it was impossible to de-
termine whether Schiller, who never mentioned
them in any of his writings or letters, had consulted
Rousseau's and Burney's works.

Schiller lacked the background to understand
Kirnberger's highly technical *Die Kunst des reinen
Satzes*. Kirnberger's influence came not from this
work, as Knudsen states,[4] but from Sulzer's *Allgemeine Theorie*, for which Kirnberger wrote many of
the musical articles. Although Schiller undoubtedly
conversed with Herder and Wieland about music,
we have no record of what was said; his letters to and
from Goethe, Reichardt, and Zelter deal with
practical rather than philosophical musical topics;
and his musical aesthetics are different from Kant's.
We must therefore conclude that Sulzer's *Allgemeine
Theorie* and Körner's letters were the two strongest

influences on Schiller's philosophical writings about
music, and a full understanding of his aesthetic ideas
requires explanation of Körner's musical background
and the circumstances surrounding the musical
articles in Sulzer's work.

After Schiller left Dresden for Weimar he maintained a correspondence with Körner which was
terminated only by the poet's death. These letters
are a basic source for the genesis of most of Schiller's
aesthetic ideas as well as for many of his informal
observations on music.

Körner's influence on Schiller has aroused contro-
versial discussion. Friedlaender attacked what he
felt to be his adverse influence by remarking that he
was a 'bungling dilettante' and 'less musical than
Schiller himself,' quoting his opinions of Haydn
out of context as evidence for these statements,
whereas Knudsen defended Körner because he was
Schiller's friend, had taught him much in Dresden,
and was the closest musical adviser at hand for the
poet.[5]

Körner had studied philology, philosophy, mathe-
matics, and science at the University of Leipzig. At
his home in Dresden he entertained most of the important musical figures of the time – Naumann,
Hiller, Paër, Zelter, and even Mozart when he was
on his way to Berlin in 1789. Not a trained composer, Körner's musical activities were limited to
singing bass, composing simple songs, and talking
about the aesthetics of music, yet he was familiar
with the arts of counterpoint, composition, acoustics,
and instrument making. His musical tastes, though

somewhat nationalistic, were rather broad, for he shared Schiller's high opinion of Zumsteeg and Zelter and esteemed the music of Gluck, Haydn, Mozart, and 'Bach,' most probably Carl Philipp Emanuel – the four greatest German composers of the second half of the eighteenth century.[6]

The principal reason for Schiller's friendship with and reliance on Körner has not been explained by previous students of Schiller's musical life: Körner was a man of wide general cultivation in a period when virtually all composers had limited intellectual outlooks. He possessed also a broad understanding of drama, poetry, aesthetics, and history, topics in which Schiller was also interested. The only other musical figures to whom he could have turned before 1796 were Zumsteeg, whom he considered to have 'more genius than culture,' and Reichardt, toward whom he had a strong personal antipathy dating from 1789 which was to explode in the *Xenienkampf* of 1796.

Schiller, however, began to share his musical ideas with Goethe after 1794 and after 1796 with Zelter, whom he felt superior to Körner in practical musical matters. Although he still continued to discuss music with Körner, he pursued an extremely independent course, for as his musical circles widened and his experiences in music grew deeper and broader, he became increasingly independent of Körner's ideas. In many of Körner's later letters one gets the impression that he is more often agreeing with Schiller's opinions than guiding his musical development.

Since the *Allgemeine Theorie* influenced Schiller's aesthetic ideas so strongly, we should examine the nature of its musical articles. When Sulzer began his great work in 1756, he knew little about music and sought a musical collaborator who shared his ideas. He soon discarded Agricola, Quantz, and Marpurg, and finally chose Kirnberger. Sulzer had to edit not only the musical articles but also Kirnberger's magnum opus, *Die Kunst des reinen Satzes*, because its author was unable to express himself in writing. Unfortunately the two could not agree on the meaning of many words, and Kirnberger disapproved of Sulzer's moralistic views on art and his thinking of music only in connection with poetry, pantomine, and dance. The result was that Kirnberger handed over many of his articles (most probably drafts) to J. A. P. Schulz, who described his work as 'contributing the materials for a series of articles which Sulzer then worked up and gave their final form.'

We know that Schiller was conversant with Sulzer's work. Knudsen remarks that the students at the Karlsschule 'secretly' read it, whereas Wagner states that lectures on it were given there. After his flight from Stuttgart Schiller requested several books from his future brother-in-law Reinwald, among them Sulzer's 'philosophische Schriften.' These, therefore, explain Gross' statement that Sulzer's influence on Schiller is most pronounced in his most significant work on aesthetics, the *Briefe über die ästhetische Erziehung des Menschen.*[7]

In the twenty-second of these letters, the only one

in which music receives more than a passing mention, Schiller echoes Sulzer's ideas on the union of the arts and goes beyond him in postulating that the boundaries between them be dissolved:

> The more general the spirit and the less limited the tendency which is given to our feelings through a given art and through a given product of this genre, the more noble is this art and the product is superior. One can look for this in works from the different arts and with different works in the same art.

And further:

> Music in its loftiest exaltation must become shape, and act upon us with the tranquil power of antiquity; the plastic and graphic arts must become music, and move us through their immediate sensuous presence; poetry in its most perfect development must, like musical art, take powerful hold of us, but at the same time, like plastic art, surround us with quiet clarity . . . Perfect style in any art . . . [is] capable of removing the characteristic limitations of that art, without however removing its specific excellence, and of lending it a more useful character by a wise employment of its proper nature.

This statement is clear when one understands that Schiller was preoccupied with form as the basis for evaluating the fine arts, but *Form* meant many things to him. Whereas the object of the sense impulse (*sinnlicher Trieb*) is life and of the form impulse shape, both are synthesized through the 'play impulse' into a 'living shape' which is equivalent to beauty. Schiller uses as a concrete analogy the idea of a statue: as long as we think merely about its shape the statue is 'lifeless, mere abstraction;' as long as we think merely about its 'life' it is shapeless and a mere impression; but 'only as the form of something lives in our sensation, and its life takes form in our under-standing, is it living shape, and this will everywhere be the case where we judge it to be beautiful,' and form is also 'an image of the infinite.'[9]

Schiller gives musical form a similarly mystical meaning in one of his most important critical essays in which he discusses music:

> Every beautiful harmony of form, tone, and light which delights the aesthetic sense satisfies at the same time the moral sense; every consistency with which lines follow each other in space or tones follow each other in time is a natural symbol of the inner harmony of the spirit with itself and the customary coherence of action with feeling, and in the beautiful harmony of a painting or piece of music there is the even more beautiful [harmony] of an ethically disposed soul.'[10]

This same idea is poetically expressed in 'Die Künst-ler:'

Schon sieht man Schöpfungen aus Schöpfungen
  erstehen,
Aus Harmonien Harmonie.

Schiller refused to engage in any 'form versus
content' controversies because he regarded these as
merely an 'entertaining game:' 'where the content
must be judged according to the form, there is no
content at all.'[11] Form, in Schiller's mind, was not
connected with the material side of music:

> If you take all form from music it loses all its
> aesthetic but not its musical power.
>   If you take all its substance away and retain only
> its pure part [form], it loses both its aesthetic and
> musical effect and becomes merely an object for
> the understanding.[12]

Form for Schiller did not necessarily mean technique,
a device which he regarded as necessary to an end:
'Freedom in appearance is indeed the foundation of
beauty, but *technique* is the necessary condition of our
representation of freedom.' Technique must appear to
be determined from the nature of the object and
seems strange when it is not an outgrowth of the
object. A mechanic can build a musical instrument:
it can be pure technique without claiming to be
beautiful. 'Autonomy in technique, freedom in
artistic correctness' is to be the artist's goal. There
is similarly an artistic and a technical form and a
difference between the objective and subjective goals
of music: 'The musician will express the emotions

of the form. This is the objective goal of music, whereas the subjective goal is, through technical means, to carry out every objective goal and thus ennoble the taste.' Schiller also distinguishes between 'Kunst' and 'schöne Kunst' and forbids the exchanging of technical with aesthetic rules.[13]

Although Abert's statement that for Schiller 'only form . . . raises music to the rest of the fine arts' is wide of the mark, Hohenemser's statement gives a clear idea of what Schiller meant by form: in opposition to the material (*e.g.*, marble, words, tones), form is not an external but the most internal matter without which a work of art is worthless. Babbitt remarks that Schiller's idea of form is essentially an inner form, 'not the mere outer form or technique that has been so often offered in art and literature as a substitute for it,' and defines this inner form as

> . . . the imposition on the raw material of experience of some pattern that has been apprehended with the imagination . . . the imagination is in the service of the power in man that consciously and with reference to some sound model sets bounds to limitless expression.

But he adds the warning that 'when one passes from outer to inner form one enters into a region of imponderables that eludes both rules and scientific measurement.'[14] Bruford explains the difference between *Formtrieb* and *Stofftrieb* as 'the pull . . . towards 'form,' the mental forming of experience' as opposed to 'the drive of the senses . . . the craving for experience through the senses,'[15] but in contrast to this statement I consider *Form* the aesthetic exigencies and *Stoff* the technical requirements of a given work of art, as the following explanation will show.

Schiller did not regard form as synonymous with structure, but as a *Gestalt*, when he remarked 'if you take all form from music it loses all its aesthetic but not its musical power.' Musical power exists in the sense of what Dent has perceptively called a physiological stimulus,[16] of which Tchaikovsky's last three symphonies and Rakhmaninov's concertos are excellent examples; yet such works lack the *Gestalt* inherent in the best works of Mozart and Beethoven. A great composer's style-traits are most readily discernible in his lesser works, for in his greatest compositions the listener is so overwhelmed by the *Gestalt* that only through familiarity with the work in question and a deliberate focusing of the mind on technical details can he direct his attention to the *Stoff* of a masterpiece.

The remainder of Schiller's statement on form, that form may exist without its musical materials, is a paradox: the *Gestalt* is independent of its musical materials, but music cannot exist without some kind of physically perceptible sound. His statement is actually a refutation of the Euclidean axiom that the whole is equal to the sum of its parts, for the *Gestalt* is greater than the sum of its technical factors, form is not identical with structure, and the aesthetician is not to be concerned exclusively with technique but with the glorious unity and effect of the entire work.

An innumerable number of musicians and writers on music have considered the stirring of the emotions to be the highest duty of this art. Two statements by Schiller's immediate predecessors need be cited: C. P. E. Bach's oft-quoted remark that 'A musician cannot move others unless he too is moved,' and the comment in Sulzer that 'a composition which does not arouse emotions is not a piece of genuine music.'[17] Knudsen believed that Schiller stated the essence of his musical aesthetics in his letter to Körner of 3 February 1794: 'The musician will express the emotions of the form,' and in the poet's essay on Matthisson's poetry he expresses it thus:

> The whole effect of music (as a fine and not merely agreeable art) [is] the inner moving of the spirit through analogous externals to accompany and to illustrate . . . If only the composer and the landscape painter will penetrate into the secret of every rule which governs the inner movement of the human heart, and will study the analogy which takes place between these movements of the spirit and certain other phenomena, thus he will rise from a depicter of common nature to a true painter of souls. From the realm of the arbitrary he enters into the realm of the necessary, and can appear not on the side of the plastic arts which depict the *external* man, but on the side of the poet who takes the *inner* man as his object.[18]

Several years earlier he expressed the same idea in his statement that 'music overcame the rough destroyer of Baghdad [Tamerlane] where Mengs and Corregio would have exhausted all their creative arts in vain . . The path of the ear is the most direct and closest to our hearts.'[19] He ascribes similar powers to music in one of his last works, the occasional drama *Die Huldigung der Künste*, in the words spoken by the allegorical figure representing music.

Despite Schiller's praise of the emotional effects of music, he often distrusted it. Since music, if it is to be successful, must stir up the emotions, the question arises whether the listener is morally better or worse after his musical experiences. Music, according to Kirnberger and Schulz, 'is and by its nature can be nothing else than an expression of emotions or a portrayal of the feelings of a soul set in motion or abandoned by them,' and such a statement explains Schiller's comment that 'in the beautiful harmony of a piece of music there is the even more beautiful [harmony] of an ethically disposed soul.'[20]

His fundamental objection to music was that it was perceived through the senses, not through the intellect. Music could produce 'lively feelings' but it was extremely difficult for the listener to make a sudden transition from 'deep musical enjoyment' to 'abstract thought,' and 'even the most etherial [*sic*] music, by reason of its matter, has a closer affinity with the senses than true aesthetic feeling allows.'[21]

In his *Schema über den Dilettantismus* (1799) Schiller discussed music from only two standpoints: music in performance or in sensuous effect. His inclusion of the dance and landscape gardening with poetry, theatre, architecture, music, and the pictorial arts parallels the 'fine arts' curriculum of the Karlsschule, and the emphasis there on music as a performing art may well have influenced Schiller's views on the technical side of musical execution. In the *Schema* he listed the arts in a series of parallel columns under which he mentions both their strong and weak values, with music discussed as follows:

Music: Composition, performance.

For the individual person, advantages: Passing time with a certain serious purpose in mechanical application. Improvement of the feelings.

For the individual person, disadvantages: Emptiness of thought. Sensuality.

In general, advantages: Sociability and momentary disinterested communication.

In general, disadvantages: Bad neighborliness. Emptiness.

In Germany, formerly: A greater influence on emotional life through portable stringed instruments. Medium of *galanterie*.

In Germany, at present: Strumming.

Abroad: A special case in Italy, where the greater amount of singing among the people more strongly inhibits bungling.[22]

His views of the technical side of music can be easily explained: strumming is simply bad playing, and he doubtlessly compared the playing of the members of his circle with the performances by Streicher, Hässler, and the touring virtuosi who passed through

Weimar, and the opera in Mannheim and Weimar
with his memories of the splendid performances in
Karl Eugen's musical theatre and the operatic productions at the Karlsschule. He had no first-hand
knowledge of the level or amount of vocal performances in Italy, but probably based his statement
on Goethe's remarks about his trips there, Heinse's
novels, and his memories of the Italian singers at
Karl Eugen's court. The clavichords rather than
the bowed stringed instruments, or the harps and
lyres of antiquity, were probably the 'portable
stringed instruments' which so strongly influenced
emotional states; Schiller may have been thinking
of Streicher's performances in the darkened room in
Mannheim, and the literature for the clavichord is
almost exclusively emotional, *empfindsam*, and intended to affect the listener's spirits.

In Chapter 1 we saw that music for Schiller was a
means of social intercourse and relaxation. *Hausmusik* was an affair in which amateurs participated,
and few guests at a musical evening remained silent
during the group singing. The almost universal
regard for music as a social accomplishment is
reflected in his remark that music was an aid to
galanterie, which is not music in the *galanter Stil* but
the eighteenth-century concept of formal politeness,
especially on the French model. 'Bad neighborliness' could easily have been professional jealousy,
disputes over interpretation, or the impatience of a
musical group with its less capable performers.

Although Schiller does not emphasize 'sensuality'
and 'emptiness' in his *Schema* as particularly injurious

drawbacks, in other essays he regards these as the most serious disadvantages of music. We have seen, in his essay on Matthisson's poetry, that he limited his praise to music 'as a fine and not merely agreeable art.' He sharply attacked 'agreeable' music, which merely charmed or delighted without ennobling or elevating. Schiller had a definite hierarchy of aesthetic values: the agreeable, the good, the sublime, and the beautiful, with only the latter two properly artistic, since the *agreeable* was not worthy to be considered as art and the *good* was not the purpose of art. In 'Über Anmut und Würde' he stated the conflict between the 'agreeable' and the 'dignified': 'There is an exciting and a restful charm. The first borders on fascination of the senses, and the satisfaction of this can, if not restrained by dignity, easily degenerate into desire,' and these opposites parallel the 'energizing' and the 'melting' beauty he describes in the fifteenth letter of the *ästhetische Erziehung*.[23] Whereas Kant, Sulzer, and Herder accepted and even welcomed 'agreeable' music, Schiller was hostile to it, as witness his attack on 'modern' music:

The music of the moderns seems remarkably aimed only toward sensuality and thus flatters the dominating taste which wants only to be agreeably tickled, not affected, not powerfully stirred, nor exalted. All sweet melodiousness is therefore preferred, and if there is an even greater noise in the concert hall, suddenly everyone becomes all ears when a sentimental passage is played. An almost animal expression of sensuality then usually

appears on all faces, the intoxicated eyes swim, the
open mouth is lustful, a voluptuous trembling
seizes the whole body, the breath is rapid and
short; soon all the symptoms of intoxication
appear as a clear indication that the senses are
running riot but that the spirit or the principle of
freedom has fallen prey to the force of sensual
impressions. All these feelings, I say, are excluded
from art through a noble and manly taste because
they please only the *feelings*, with which art has
nothing to do.[24]

This diatribe excellently illustrates the shift in
musical aesthetics between the middle and later
years of the eighteenth century. Brown, Benjamin
Franklin, and Avison complained that music was
becoming too harmonically and contrapuntally
elaborate: in Franklin's words, the composers were
only 'admirable at pleasing *practiced* ears, and know
how to delight *one another*.'[25] Around 1770, on the
other hand, attacks on modern music took a new
direction, as the following quotation by Kirnberger
and Schulz shows:

Much has been gained ... through melismatic
ornaments in songs and new harmonic resources,
but on the other hand so much misuse of ornaments and freedom in harmony has been made
that at present music is in danger of complete
degeneration ... Recently music owed much in
beautiful and very flexible genius and feelings to

the Italians, but also voluptuousness and melodies which say nothing and merely tickle the ear.

And Dies virtually paraphrases Schiller's attack in describing Italian operatic melodies, which 'tickle the public's fancy and set its emotions to work' but are 'empty of inner content because the intellect on closer inspection finds little, often only trivial, nourishment that shows not the slightest trait of ennoblement.'[26]

The Italian music under discussion was not the Neapolitan music of the early years of the century by Pergolesi, Leo, Vinci, and the other demigods in Rousseau's musical pantheon, nor even the revitalized *opera seria* of Jommelli and Traëtta, but the music of a newer school of composers: Cimarosa, Guglielmi, Anfossi, Paisiello, and their imitators. One is reminded of the attacks on this Italian music by the two Mozarts, Beethoven, Spohr, and Wagner in Germany and by Berton and Boïeldieu in France, and only the most chauvinistic will deny that a certain amount of professional envy and jealousy lay behind their strictures. Yet the fluency of Italian melody during Schiller's lifetime and afterwards threatened to drive the music of the more serious composers out of the concert halls and opera houses. We need only to recall the impact of Rossini on nineteenth-century France. Yet unlike the musical foes of the contemporaneous Italian opera, Schiller did not attack this music on nationalistic grounds.

His hostility toward 'agreeable' music also stemmed from his ideas, stated even in his earliest

philosophical writings, on the moral utility and effect
of music. The kernel of his attack on 'modern' music
is not that it is bad *qua* music, but that its influence
leads to a 'voluptuous,' 'sensual,' and 'intoxicated'
state of mind rather than to a 'noble and manly
taste.' Schiller has been compared with Liszt as a
'preacher' about art; [27] it is sufficient here to state
that his views of the moral (not in the merely Puritan
sense) effect of art anticipated the ideas of Beethoven,
Schumann, Wagner, and Nietzsche. Art that is
merely agreeable is, in Schiller's canon, not only
aesthetically unworthy but also meretricious and
even pernicious; later composers, especially Berlioz
and Liszt, advanced the corollary that great art must
carry a 'message.'

Schiller's aesthetic views on music as a fine art
continued into his opinions on specific musical
genres, composers, and compositions, as we can see
from his writings, letters, and informal conversations. He refrained from citing concrete illustrations of his musical ideas because, as he explained,
'what in general is perfectly true suffers limitation in
[the citation of] each individual case,' [28] but informally he made several pronouncements on actual
music which are basically consistent with his
aesthetic judgments and also reflect the critical spirit
of his era.

Hohenemser's statement that Schiller was attracted
chiefly to opera because of his dramatic interests and
to song because of his poetic activity explains his
limited interest in instrumental music. [29] Even
though Schiller personally loved clavier music and

displayed in his metaphors and dramatic characterizations more than a casual acquaintance with musical
instruments, the few statements about such music
which do occur in his writings are rather vague and
indefinite,* but do not manifest the studied indiffer-
ence or even hostility to instrumental music characteristic of Sulzer, Brown, or Herder.[30]

The best instrumental music Schiller was able to
hear was clavier music. In all likelihood Streicher
introduced him to C. P. E. Bach's expressive music,
and one of his few written references to a specific
composer, even though the two men soon quarreled,
contains high praise of the playing and the compositions of Johann Wilhelm Hässler, who 'played like
a master,' 'composes very well,' and 'has much that
is original and very much fire.'[31] Schiller undoubtedly heard Hässler's 'solos' of 1785 and the sonatas of
1779, works which deserve to rank below only the
best keyboard compositions of C. P. E. Bach,
Mozart, and Haydn. Hässler is at his best in 'Sturm
und Drang' allegros and melancholy soliloquies,
such as the F minor andantino in his third 'solo.'

No information, however, is available concerning
the clavier music owned and played by the ladies in
Schiller's family circle. Such amateur musicians of

---

* An excellent example of Schiller's vagueness in using instrumental
terminology can be seen in his review of Johann Matthisson's
poem 'Abendlandschaft' when he states that a 'beautiful sonata'
could be made on this 'Lied' (SA, XVI, 263-64). Schiller also uses
the word 'Modulation,' but not in its musical context. Concerning
Mainland's interpretation of this review, see my comments in the
Bibliographical Essay to Chapter III.

the period played music ranging from simple mi-
nuets, murkies, and marches to the easier sonatas
and variations by C. P. E. Bach, Mozart, Haydn,
Hässler, and Clementi. Clavier music was the best
instrumental music Schiller was able to hear, because
the chamber music in his environment was almost
exclusively *Hausmusik* for amateurs; the best
orchestra he could have heard was the student
orchestra at the Karlsschule with its limited repertoire, though he may have attended performances
of the Collegium Musicum in Jena; and the *Harmoniemusik* he encountered in Bauerbach and Weimar was
functional music intended only to divert its players
and hearers.

Two instruments aroused Schiller's interest because of their sound-qualities, independent of the
music written for them. As a child he was delighted
by organ music, and in his essay 'Über Anmut und
Würde' he mentioned the importance of the organ
in creating an atmosphere of solemnity.[32] Unfortunately the period between J. S. Bach and Mendelssohn produced no organ music of any account. At
Dresden Schiller heard the glass harmonica at
Körner's house and was so captivated by it that in
Der Geisterseher he gave this instrument a major role
in establishing an atmosphere of mystery during the
seance.

On the other hand, Schiller took a lively interest
in vocal music, which was more popular than
instrumental music in all of the communities where
he resided as well as among the members of his
intellectual coterie. He had only a very limited

acquaintance with church music – Pietistic hymns learned from his mother and concerted Te Deums heard at the Karlsschule – and seems to have been more attracted by Catholic than Protestant church music. Whereas in *Die Räuber* (II, 3) he referred to the 'grässliche Musik' of the (Protestant) psalm-singing before Roller's impending execution, Schiller praised Catholic church music in *Maria Stuart* (I, 6), where Mortimer describes the 'music of Heaven' which he heard in Rome and which helped bring about his conversion:

> als ich ins Innre nun
> Der Kirchen trat und die Musik der Himmel
> Herunterstieg und der Gestalten Fülle
> Verschwenderisch aus Band und Decke quoll . . .

Schiller's knowledge of Catholic church music may have come from many sources: Herder at least mentioned Palestrina, Leo, and Durante in his writings; Karoline von Wolzogen had, according to Körner, at least the opportunity to hear 'lovely church music' by Hasse in Dresden; Goethe glorified 'spiritual songs in the Latin language' which 'speak to the deepest and best ideas in man and let him . . . feel in a living manner his likeness to the Deity' in *Wilhelm Meister;* Heinse wrote on Catholic church music although he lumped Palestrina and Pergolesi together; and Destouches, then Schiller's theatrical composer, was a Catholic.[33] Although Schiller directed several inquiries to Körner during the writing of *Maria Stuart* concerning details of Catholic ritual, he asked no questions about its music. It is not improbable that these various encomia of Catholic religious music are among the significant anticipations of the German Romantic interest in Catholicism, from which not even Mendelssohn and Schumann were totally immune.

During Schiller's youth choral music was infrequently sung in Germany, but the rise of Freemasonry brought about a renewed interest in group singing, as witness the numerous collections of Masonic works of which Mozart's Masonic music (K. 468, 471, and 623) and the priests' chorus in Act II of *Die Zauberflöte* are the greatest examples. Schiller's 'An die Freude,' especially in Hurka's setting, was a favorite of the lodges and appeared in several collections of Masonic songs. Dissatisfied with the texts of songs for group singing, the poet wished to have a 'more elevated text' to prevent their falling into the 'dull, prosaic style' of Masonic songs, the fate of 'all social songs which do not have a poetic subject.'[34] 'Die vier Weltalter,' 'An die Freunde,' and 'Das Siegesfest' are among the poems which he wrote to be sung chorally at Goethe's Mittwochkränzchen, and such settings of Schiller's poems as Schubert's 'An den Frühling' and Mendelssohn's 'Des Menschen Würde' were staples of the nineteenth-century *Männerchöre*.

At Weimar Herder demonstrated his interest in the oratorio by translating Handel's *Messiah* and *Alexander's Feast* for performances in 1780, but while Schiller was there between 1787 and 1805 oratorios were neglected. He knew Haydn's *The*

Seasons only by name but was able to hear a performance of his *Creation* on New Year's Eve, 1800.
His remark to Körner about this work was quite
severe: 'I had little pleasure because it is a charac-
terless mishmash.'[35]

In retrospect it is easy to understand Schiller's poor
opinion of Haydn's masterpiece. He preferred works
of a unified character to the mixture of styles in *The
Creation*, which includes the strange modulations
of the 'Representation of Chaos,' the tone-paintings
of natural scenes which dangerously skirt the naive
(the bird-songs) or the ridiculous (the celebrated
contrabassoon entrance in the bass aria in Part II),
and 'learned' contrapuntal choruses like the double
fugue which concludes Part II of the oratorio.
Furthermore, Schiller had undoubtedly never heard
a note of Handel's or J. S. Bach's choral music, or
even the popular and sentimental *Der Tod Jesu* by
K. H. Graun. Unfamiliarity with a genre new to
him, and in all likelihood a none too secure performance, no doubt contributed to his bewilderment
and adverse reaction to *The Creation*.

Most of what Schiller knew about Haydn derived
from his correspondence with Körner. Since the
cornerstone of Friedlaender's denigration of Schiller's musical counsellor is Körner's alleged low
opinion of Haydn, one need only examine Körner's
correspondence to find out that Friedlaender quoted
his anti-Haydn remarks out of context. In his
description of the 'German school' of composers in
1794 Körner singled out for special praise C. P. E.
Bach, Gluck, Haydn, and Mozart, and commented

that 'there is more dignity than grace [a reference to 'Anmut und Würde?'] in the character of German music.' However, Körner knew that Schiller would be more interested in composers of vocal music than in even the greatest of instrumental composers. This explains his recommendation: 'If you need a composer for *Die Malteser* I would propose Haydn, but much rather Salieri, if he understands German.' One should recall that, largely on the strength of *Tarare*, Salieri was regarded in 1797 in Germany as the greatest composer of serious opera since Gluck. In later letters Körner stated an even stronger reason for not recommending Haydn as a vocal composer:

> Becker wants ['Sehnsucht'] set to music, and would like to ask Haydn about it. I only doubt whether he understands a good poem, as he has always lived in poor poetic company, and therefore have recommended Zelter, Sterkel, or Hurka.

And, in replying to Schiller's criticism of *The Creation*, he remarked that 'Haydn is a skillful artist, but lacks inspiration. For the musician there is much in his works to be studied, but the whole [effect] is coldness.'[36] Seifert, however, states that Körner was not completely opposed to Haydn's music, for he heard 'many chamber works and symphonies' of his in Dresden and performed much of his music in the Körnerschen Singanstalt which he founded on Zelter's advice.[37] In fairness to Körner, we should also remember that only in recent years have our musical 'tastemakers' really understood Haydn's musical significance.

Most of Schiller's musical opinions concerned opera, a form with which he had been acquainted since his childhood. His judgments were based not on prejudices but on some knowledge of most of the operatic literature of the time. We have seen that before 1783 he enjoyed the opera at Ludwigsburg, though his pleasure was more in the spectacle than in the music; that he participated as an actor in the prologue to Sacchini's *Callirroë;* that he virtually lost himself in delight with Georg Benda's *Ariadne auf Naxos;* and that he admired Holzbauer's *Günther von Schwarzburg.* Yet one of his earliest recorded opinions of a specific opera, Holzbauer's *Die Zerstörung von Carthago,* a setting of a libretto by Metastasio, is quite critical:

> The poetry and music affected me equally little, and I believe that my opinion corresponds with the general view. Unfortunately I am no connoisseur, and also as an amateur I could not pretend to speak of it. The production went well.[38]

This opera is the *Dido* mentioned in *Kabale und Liebe.* When Hofmarschall von Kalb announces its impending performance (III, 2) he speaks of the fireworks in the stage spectacle rather than the music.

These statements mark the onset of Schiller's anti-opera period. He was soon to call the grand opera 'an Auto da Fé for nature and the art of poetry;' to comment on the 'unnaturalness of opera,' which affected him 'as one who comes to the city for the first time;' and to state in 1787 that *Don Carlos* was his best theatrical work which he had written 'without the help of spectacle and operatic décor.'[39] The main reason for his rejection of opera during his stay in Mannheim and Dresden, as Buchwald has remarked, was that the grand *opera seria* was part of a 'Baroque' culture against which he was in revolt.[40] The artificiality and unreality of the genre and his resentment at his treatment by Karl Eugen contributed to his disdain for opera. 'Die schlimmen Monarchen' of 1782, a poem 'dedicated,' one might say, to the opera-loving Duke, contains anti-operatic references to 'Theaterminotaure,' the stage effect of 'Siegespauken,' and the 'Gaukler in dem Opernhaus.' He was not alone in his attacks on the grand Italianate opera, for Gottsched had called it an 'Unkunst;' Sulzer criticized the 'strange mixture of great and small, beautiful and tasteless;' and both Hölty and Matthias Claudius considered opera to be superficial, artificial, and unnatural.[41]

During the 1790s Schiller's attitude toward opera underwent a gradual change, chiefly because of the influence of the Weimar court theatre under Goethe's direction. Although the productions were not characterized by the excellent orchestral and scenic resources and the full-time professional singers for all the vocal parts typical of performances in such major operatic centres as Berlin, Munich, and Vienna, the operas were quite carefully rehearsed in Weimar by the standards of the time, and the repertoire was of high quality. All of Mozart's

major operas except *Idomeneo* were given as well as
the better operas of Dittersdorf, Paisiello, Cimarosa,
and many Italian, Austrian, and German composers
once highly regarded but now forgotten. Even a
few French *opéras comiques* were given in translation.
Opera, in fact, was more popular than drama, a
circumstance which provoked peevish remarks from
both Goethe and Schiller. The audience, which
included not only members of the court circles but
also professional men, artists, army officers, and
professors and students from the University of Jena,
was one of the best in Germany.

A revival of Gluck's *Iphigenia auf Tauris* in 1796
won Schiller whole-heartedly to opera. Goethe
asked him to supervise its rehearsals; Schiller agreed,
but replied 'as you know, in musical matters I have...
little competence and insight... with my best will
and ability I will be of little service to you.' The
memory of the production of this opera remained
with Schiller four years later, when he wrote Goethe
that 'the music was so heavenly that I was moved to
tears at the rehearsal, despite the foolishness and
distraction of the singers,' and Körner that 'Never
has so pure and lovely a music affected me... it is a
world of harmony which presses directly to the soul
and dissolves in sweet exalted melancholy,' sentiments which Schiller later had the allegorized figure
of Music repeat in *Die Huldigung der Künste*.[42]

As early as 1787 Schiller asked Wilhelm von
Wolzogen to return to him an unnamed piece by
Gluck which he had lent him before being able to
copy it[43], and around 1790 the poet was delighted

with an ariette from *La Rencontre imprévue;* thus he had been acquainted with Gluck's lighter music for several years. Yet not until he heard *Iphigenia* did he have a yardstick by means of which he could measure operatic greatness. He soon stated his new beliefs concerning opera to Goethe:

> I have always had a certain confidence in the opera, that in it, as in the choruses of the old Bacchic festivals, the tragedy can unravel in a noble form. In the opera one is really released from all slavish copying of nature, and only in this way, under the name of indulgence, can it avoid the theatrical ideal. The opera arises from the power of music, and through a free harmonious charming of the senses the spirit [is elevated] to a beautiful conception; pathos is also given free rein because the music accompanies it and the marvelous, which is tolerated here, must necessarily be made subordinate to the plot.[44]

Iphigenia auf Tauris is Gluck's most consistent major opera. Dramatically it is a tight work with diversions held to a minimum; the ballets further the action rather than provide opportunities for display and spectacle; 'music for music's sake,' even an overture, is absent; economy of means is a striking characteristic; and, most important, the opera is uncompromising in its unity of style without any relaxation of the nobility of sentiment through any diversion which would have catered to popular taste. Schiller was also familiar with Euripides' *Iphigenia* (in translation) and Goethe's drama on the same subject; thus Gluck's opera appealed to him on literary and aesthetic as well as on musical grounds. He had finally found the work which appealed to his aesthetic sensibilities: the expression of the emotions of the form; an 'energizing' rather than a 'melting' beauty; a dissolution of the boundaries between music, poetry, and the stage; a topic from the Grecian mythology which he had so often celebrated in his poems; and a nobly dignified work without concessions to sensual tastes.

Schiller's high opinion of Gluck explains not only his attack on Haydn's *Creation* but also his lack of appreciation for Mozart's operas, the only examples of this composer's music Schiller probably ever heard. He attended a performance of *Die Zauberflöte* and later remarked to Goethe that 'you are missing something by being away during this musical week,' but discussed Gern's performance of Sarastro rather than the music; he at least knew of *Così fan tutte;* he planned to attend a performance of *Le Nozze di Figaro;* he twice thought that *Don Giovanni* would be suitable for a ballad and had attended a concert performance of it in Jena; and he complained that a production of *La Clemenza di Tito* 'took the theatre away from us.'[45] He was obviously quite conversant with Mozart's operas. Goethe and Körner both tried to interest him further in these works. In answering Schiller's letter containing his essay on opera, Goethe remarked:

The hope you entertain of the opera you may have recently seen realized in the highest degree in *Don Giovanni*, but this work stands alone, and because of Mozart's death all prospect of the production of anything similar is at an end.

Körner had entertained Mozart in Dresden during his journey to Berlin in 1789 and told Schiller that 'Mozart was perhaps the only one who could be as great in the comic as in the tragic,' but Seifert is overly speculative when he says that 'it is definitely to be supposed that he had commented on Mozart to Schiller when one considers that he said much about many insignificant composers.'[46]

Schiller made, however, only one statement about the music in Mozart's operas. During his visit to Weimar the music student Schlömilch, whom we have earlier seen as a probable emissary from Bernhard Anselm Weber in Berlin, discussed music with Schiller. In the course of the conversation someone praised *Don Giovanni* and especially the way Mozart used the trombones in Act II, but Schiller terminated the discussion by remarking that Gluck had anticipated Mozart's employment of the trombones in depicting the supernatural and expressing regret that Mozart's operas were superseding Gluck's works.[47]

The mixture of styles in Mozart's music probably caused Schiller to underestimate this composer. 'His music could and still can be perceived on two levels. He was quite aware that the charm of the music would speak to the uninitiated audience, and that, at the same time, its sophistication would delight the discriminating ears of the connoisseurs,'[48] but Schiller, who had already attacked the 'agreeable' and 'modern' music of his time, was unable to recognize Mozart's transformation and transfiguration of the operatic practice of his day. In his mature dramas Schiller avoided the mixing of comic and serious elements, for he was careful to separate the high spirits of *Wallensteins Lager* from the serious tragedy of the other two dramas in the trilogy, and after the early 'Die Rache der Musen' his only other humorous poems are the acidly sardonic *Xenien*. Schiller was impressed with Sarastro's role in *Die Zauberflöte* because it is serious throughout and owes much to Gluck. The dominance of music in Mozart's operas, though criticized by Herder,[49] might have offended Schiller had he been cognizant of it; but this same apparent defect occurs in an opera which he had previously praised highly, Holzbauer's *Günther von Schwarzburg*. Not the 'too many notes' in Mozart's music about which Joseph II complained, but its mixture of styles, most probably occasioned Schiller's disparagement of it.

Toward the end of his life Schiller believed that the most effective music was the simplest. In 'Anmut und Würde' he had previously given a virtual recipe for the creation of a solemn effect:

In music solemnity is produced through slow, uniform, strong tones; the strength awakens and braces the spirit, the slowness lengthens the satisfaction, and the uniformity of the rhythm lets impatience perceive no end to it. Solemnity does not insignificantly support the impression of greatness and exaltation, and is used with great success in religious services and mysteries.

He subsequently amplified this statement in a conversation with Christel von Wurmb:

The peoples of antiquity achieved such an astonishing effect with their music because it was *simple*. Its single chords pressed to the heart and stirred it. A uniform sound [gleichförmiger Ton] can set men to the highest degree of exertion... how much more...must these feelings be affected when these...occur in the fullness of harmony. Apparently this is the basis for which in every kind of consecration, for example in Masonic lodges, this type of music is chosen, and why the ancients, before they advanced to single combat in the arena, had the trumpets sound single notes.[50]

Simplicity as a hallmark of musical merit was not an original opinion, for it recurs countless times in the writings of eighteenth-century musical aestheticians and is the basic thesis of Gluck's preface to *Alceste*, a document which Schiller would have endorsed wholeheartedly. He liked music that was either based on a simple melody or was written in a monumentally simple style, and as a poet he was reluctant to have his texts smothered in vocal coloraturas, piano figurations, or settings which contained too much music. His idea of the strong effect of the single note as a means of musical expression casts a new light on a certain rhetorical effect in the music of his time, for in this context we can better understand the tromboned E-flats in *Die Zauberflöte*, the isolated, sustained octave Fs in the introduction to Beethoven's *Egmont* overture, and the empty fifths (with superimposed arpeggios) opening his ninth symphony.

Both Schiller's speculative and critical musical aesthetics were affected by the music he had heard, the writings of the aestheticians (especially the authors of the musical articles in Sulzer), the advice of his musical friends, and the deficiencies in his practical and theoretical background in music. His employment of terminology is often ambiguous and vague, his reasoning is frequently based on preconceived ideas and confuses the reader who is accustomed to opinions based on concrete illustrations, and his tastes were reactionary for the time, thus foreshadowing the present trend wherein many reject today's musical styles and seek aesthetic satisfaction from the established 'classics.' Yet Schiller was consistent in his ideas, especially when he had Gluck's *Iphigenia auf Tauris* as an illustration of his ideas of greatness in music.* His favorite compositions were the expressively *empfindsame* melodies of the North German clavichordists (C.P.E. Bach, Hässler), the simple melodious ariettes

* The one possible contradiction is his fondness for the aria 'Ombra adorata' from Zingarelli's *Giulietta e Romeo*. The aria, however, is not in the style of the Italian composers of the 1770s and 1780s but instead is a forerunner of the expressive melodic lines of Bellini.

of the French *opéra comique* (Dalayrac, Gluck), and
the heroic opera in a consistently monumental and
simple style.

We can also acknowledge Schiller's contributions
to the ideas of dignity in music, the importance of
this art in *Bildung* and *Kultur*, and the intentional
production of the musical masterpiece. His lofty
idealism had no small influence on the thinking of
Beethoven, Schumann, and Wagner, the earnestness
of the nineteenth-century composer, and the use of
art as a substitute for religion with a corresponding
over-idealization and humorlessness in art. The high
seriousness of the German or German-oriented
composers of the last centnry, from Beethoven
through d'Indy, has fallen into disrepute except in
Marxist circles, yet this attitude produced much fine
music, and even the poor works of this epoch are
dull rather than intentionally bad or tasteless. Bruch
and Dräsecke, as well as Beethoven, Wagner, and
Brahms, are equally products of the idealized artistic
tradition for which Schiller spoke.

Eighteen decades separate the songs Zumsteeg wrote
for the first performance of *Die Räuber* in 1781 and
the second revision of Giselher Klebe's opera, based
on this same drama. During these 181 years many
composers attempted, with varying degrees of
success, to unite their music with Schiller's poems
or dramas, with a few masterpieces surviving in the
current repertoire and others enjoying neglect or
oblivion, yet all of the music written to his texts
represents this author as seen through minds of
varying literary interests and compositional abilities
who expressed themselves in many different musical
styles.

This chapter does not contain a complete listing of
the various settings of Schiller's compositions, as
such an undertaking would be close to impossible
and a nearly complete list is cited in the article
'Schiller' in *Grove*. I have tried to fill the significant
lacunae in the previous studies based on Schiller's
works and have studied these works in chronological
order according to their medium – art-song, choral
work, opera, and program music.

1. Art-Songs

During the middle years of the eighteenth century
lyric poets were no longer content with being merely
librettists for song composers, but wanted their
works considered as independent artistic productions
and thus created for the composer the problem of
putting a text to music. On one hand, the lyric
poems became more independent and, as we have

seen in Chapter III, almost musical in themselves;
Schulz' comment on seeing Klopstock's odes:
'Komponieren soll ich das? Das ist ja schon Musik!'
is indicative of the independence lyric poetry had
attained by 1770. Conversely, the poets wished to
eliminate operatic song melodies and to return to the
simplicity of a song which would be singable without accompaniment. The idea 'Sing your songs
while composing them without using an instrument
and without thinking that a bass would be added'
deprived the composer of two areas – accompaniment and refined harmonic expression – in which he
could operate freely and independently.[1] The Lied
could not flourish until this restrictive aesthetic was
discarded.

Körner perceptively saw that the independence of
Schiller's poetry made musical settings in keeping
with the aesthetic of the time a very difficult task.
'Up to now you have never made it easy for the
musician, and many things have gotten into [your
poems] which can be better read than sung,' and
'not to destroy the melody...is a special difficulty for
the musician.'[2] Schiller's prosody created further
problems for the composer, for although only minor
complications occur in the poems definitely intended
to be sung, such as those in the dramas, adapting the
imaginative metrics and line-construction of especially his philosophical poems to such musical
exigencies as the symmetrical phrase-dominated
melody typical of the Lieder of his time proved to be
a formidable task. Such problems arose even in the
'social songs,' for Körner remarked that 'the long

lines and the construction of the strophes as a whole
do not make [the organizing of] musical periods
easy.'[3]

Most of Schiller's poetry is better read aloud than
sung, for it is too independent, not only because of
the sense of the words in the philosophical poems,
but also, as Friedlaender points out:

> Schiller's lyrics [are] more artistic than natural
> poetry, the thoughts have superiority over
> observation and experience, and the brilliance of
> Schiller's diction leaves not much more for the
> musician to say. Exactly where Goethe's poetry
> excels...Schiller's fails. The apparently impro-
> vised and only hinting [angedeutete] poem is what
> has always exercised the greatest influence on
> composers.[4]

It is interesting to see how various composers have
tried to solve this problem.

Johann Rudolf Zumsteeg was the first to set Schiller's poems to music. In a flush of youthful enthusiasm Schiller highly recommended his overture
to *Die Räuber* to Count Dalberg and in the foreword
to the second edition of this drama expressed the
hope that the texts of the songs would be forgotten
on account of Zumsteeg's music. The composer in
later life, however, was ashamed of these early
songs.[5] Schiller and Zumsteeg were friends until the
latter's death in 1802, and although Schiller strove
to interest his publisher Cotta and Goethe in him, he
appreciated him as a man and comrade rather than

as a musician, as shown in his remark 'Among the musicians [at the Karlsschule] Zumsteeg is the most skilled but has more genius than culture.'[6]

Zumsteeg's mature settings of Schiller's poems range from simple strophic melodies ('Nadowessiers Totenlied,' 'An die Freude') to the lengthy, large-scale works which were later to influence Schubert. 'Thekla' ('Der Eichwald brauset') from *Die Piccolomini*) has an independent piano prelude but an extremely simple and limited accompaniment to the vocal melody. 'Ritter Toggenburg,' one of his most famous songs, is through-composed with an accompaniment that chiefly supports the vocal line, but the right-hand part does not merely double the voice. 'Maria Stuart' is like an Italian *scena ed aria*, with considerable vocal ornamentation (especially in the andantino section) and a dramatic allegro vivace ending in which one would expect orchestral accompaniment. Most unusual is 'Die Entzückung an Laura,' which is printed on only two staves (the voice and the right-hand part occupying one stave and the bass the other) in the style of the pre-1780 Lieder which were intended to be sung by the clavier player, but is a large-scale work with ritornelli, recitatives in accompagnato style, a 'pastorale,' a melodrama with a text 'während der Musik declamiert,' and a wandering tonality which begins in A and ends in E-flat major.

Johann Friedrich Reichardt, the first major composer whom Schiller met during his Weimar-Jena period, has interested many writers because he set more of Schiller's poems than any composer except Schubert, was one of the principal founders of the nineteenth-century Lied, and quarreled with Goethe and Schiller, thus providing an important stimulus to their acerb *Xenien*. Schiller initially disliked and distrusted Reichardt when they first met in 1789, though he quietly confided his misgivings to his fiancée and to Körner, yet despite Goethe's warnings hoped to have him collaborate on *Die Horen* and the *Musenalmanach*. The collaboration soon collapsed when Reichardt attempted to set 'Der Tanz' according to its author's specifications. Schiller understood that it would be a difficult poem because it was 'in a verse-style which is not comfortable for the musician...but...what can difficulties be for the master?' and suggested a 'usual dance, only...in a more idealized manner...not everything has to be sung...some places which become philosophical can be in recitative.' He then made his friendliest remark to 'Fritz:' 'I forget that I am a pitiable layman and am speaking with a master.' Reichardt sent a draft of his setting but finally 'despaired,' as Schiller told Körner, of finishing the piece 'because it could be done only on a large scale and in full score,' a judgment in which Körner eventually concurred.[8]

Reichardt's quarrel with Goethe and Schiller, at first political in nature, became personal with the publication of their *Xenien*. Schiller instigated the personal attack and proposed to Goethe that 'he must be assailed as a musician, for he is not right in that either, and it is only fair that we follow him into his last refuge, since he made war on us in our legit-

imate territory.' Of the 74 *Xenien* which directly
attack Reichardt, three disparage his music: it is
called 'ice-cold' and 'music for the mind' in 'Gewisse
Melodien,' 'frosty and heartless' in 'Überschriften
dazu,' and in 'Der böse Geselle:'

> Dichter, bitte die Musen, vor ihm dein Lied zu
> bewahren!
> Auch dein leichtestes zieht nieder der schwere
> Gesang.

Reichardt's habit of praising his own music,
as in his review of his own compositions for the
first volume of *Die Horen* published in the first
volume of his own journal *Deutschland* (February
1796) was assailed in 'Kunstgriff:'

> Schreib die Journale nur anonym, so kannst du
> mit vollen
> Backen deine Musik loben, es merkt es kein
> Mensch.

Körner, although he admired some of Reichardt's
music, supported Schiller's attack:

> He does not lack spirit and poetic feeling, but
> he does not know enough [about] the means of
> his art as much as he chatters about it. For the
> musician his works have a poverty and dryness
> which he himself would like to sell as Classicism,
> but which really is the consequence of musical
> impotence.[9]

Yet as early as 1797, a year after the *Xenienkampf*,
Schiller's rancor toward Reichardt cooled and he was
able to speak neutrally of and even recommend some

of his compositions. After his death Reichardt wrote Charlotte to ask whether her late husband had left any unpublished poems which would be suitable for musical settings and in 1810 assembled nearly all of his compositions of Schiller's poems under the title *Schillers lyrische Gedichte in Musik gesetzt*. He sent her a copy indirectly through Christiane von Goethe.[10]

Among Reichardt's settings of Schiller's poems are such scenes from his dramas as Johanna's monologues from the prologue of Act iv of *Die Jungfrau von Orleans* and Thekla's monologues from *Die Piccolomini* and *Wallensteins Tod*, all of which were intended for concert performance and would be unsuitable for use in dramatic productions. Twenty-seven of Schiller's poems, some with two and, in the case of 'Die Ideale,' three different versions, are contained in Reichardt's collection. The vocal lines range from the simple ('Das Mädchen aus der Fremde,' 'An den Frühling') to the rather elaborate ('Die Begegnung,' 'Thekla'), with quite wide vocal ranges often demanded of the singer ('Würde der Frauen,' 'Hektors Abschied.') Several of the songs are written in the minor mode, chiefly to create a folksong-like effect ('Der Jüngling am Bache,' 'Der Alpen-jäger'). Most of the choral settings are in the style of social songs, but such choral pieces as 'Die Ideale' and 'Die Worte des Glaubens,' with its final strophe 'like a chorale,' are of high quality.

Many of Reichardt's Lieder became very popular in the early nineteenth century, and Salmen believes that they significantly contributed to the popularizing of Schiller's poetry.[11] A study of the popularizing of poetry through musical settings remains to be written, but in such an investigation Reichardt's works would occupy a prominent position. He could not only set poems in a lofty and dramatic manner but could also write the sort of 'Lieder am Clavier zu singen' which appealed to the genteel young ladies of the *Biedermeier* period, and songs in a popular style of composition later to be practiced by Silcher and his followers.

Carl Friedrich Zelter's songs first became known in Weimar when the English-born Balt Johann LaTrobe sang some at one of Hufeland's musicales in 1796. Although Goethe displayed initial reservations concerning the music of his future musical adviser, Schiller eagerly dispatched a letter to 'Herr Zelter, famous musician in Berlin' in which he invited him to write some songs for his *Musenalmanach*. Soon thereafter he sent him 'Klage des Ceres' with the comment that it might be 'too big for a vocal composition,' and 'Worte des Glaubens' with his expression of doubt concerning its lyrical quality, 'whether it can be sung I do not know, perhaps in the spirit of a church song. I leave it to your genius.'[12] 1796 was also the year of the *Xenienkampf* and the resultant break with Reichardt. Schiller no longer had the counsel of a professional musician in whom he could repose full confidence, and in 1797, after the fiasco of Körner's 'Reiterlied,' could not continue to remain wholly certain of the creative ability of his erstwhile musical counselor; neither could he apparently trust Kranz or Destouches with anything really important. When the question arose of a major

musical setting, whether of dramatic incidental
music or of an important poem, Schiller thought
first of Zelter.

The two men did not meet until 1802. Zelter's
accounts of Schiller's initial impressions of him are
conflicting; in 1823 he stated that when he played
his setting of 'Der Taucher' Schiller "leaped half
clothed at me, powerfully embraced me, and called
out with emotion, 'You are my man, you understand
me!'" whereas in 1830 he related how "Schiller
entered, only half dressed, 'This is the right way, so
must it be!'[13]" Unfortunately most of their correspondence has been lost and Zelter's informative
autobiography breaks off before his first contact
with Schiller in 1796.

Zelter set relatively few of Schiller's poems but in
the ballads displayed the most creative contemporaneous solution to the problems of the long poems
with their unusual prosody. In 'Erwartung' (called
'Im Garten') and 'Der Handschuh' Zelter used
metric changes between phrases in order to adapt
his melody to the rhythm of the prosody. The latter
ballad, called 'eine Erzählung,' is in rondo form, a
solution of the question of achieving unity in a
cursive setting of a long poem. 'Der Taucher,' on
the other hand, has a nice melody but, as Körner
pointed out, was too strophic, lacked piano interludes, and called forth the question: 'are all stanzas
to be sung through to the end?'[14] Of the remaining
poems, 'Des Mädchens Klage' is inferior to the
settings of Schubert or even Körner.

Zelter is highly regarded today not because of his

musical talent but because of his close and intimate friendship with Goethe which arose after their personal meeting in 1802, his revival of Baroque choral music (especially that of J. S. Bach) with the Berlin Singakademie, and his teaching and guiding the young Mendelssohn.

Among the composers whom Körner recommended to Schiller Friedrich Franz Hurka is significant chiefly because of Friedlaender's attacks on him as 'saccharine' and 'the Franz Abt of his time' and his undocumented statement that Schiller followed Körner's advice to send him some poems to be set to music.[15] Although Hurka was a minor talent, his settings of Schiller's songs do not deserve Friedlaender's harsh strictures and his music for 'Das Lied von der Glocke,' though very modest, is not without imaginative touches.

Of all his contemporaries who set his poems, Schiller was most critical of Johann Gottfried Naumann. He referred to his setting of 'Die Ideale' as a 'gargling exercise,' and Zelter quoted the poet's slashing attack on what may have been another version:

The first thing Schiller said to me about this composition, which thoroughly irritated him, was 'How could so famous and celebrated a man crush a poem so much, that over this constant strumming on the piano the soul of the poem should be torn to shreds, and this is what all composers do.'

On the other hand, Schiller seems to have had some personal regard for Naumann, and Seifert's statement that the poet had an 'antipathy' to the composer cannot be supported.[16] Evidently Schiller disliked the active accompaniments which were soon, in the songs of Schubert, Schumann, and Brahms, to participate equally in the creation of the Lied.

The Austrian Lied between Mozart and Schubert has been only slightly explored, but in the scattered studies of this music a few settings of Schiller's songs occur. For example, Knepler cites settings of 'Die Blumen' and 'Die Erwartung' by Nicolas Freiherr von Krufft to support his thesis that Schubert was an Austrian, rather than a German, composer.[17] Undoubtedly a considerable number of Schiller's poems were set during the two decades after his death, but they have been overshadowed by the works of Franz Schubert, who set some 31 of these poems as Lieder, some in as many as three different versions.

Schubert's interest in Schiller extended from 1811 to 1824 but he wrote only five songs to the poet's texts after 1817. In addition to the more concise poems, the lyric poems, and the songs from the dramas, Schubert also set some of the ballads and philosophical poems.

His settings of the songs from the dramas rise above their original atmospheric function and are therefore unsuitable for inclusion in staged performances of the plays. This is true not only of 'Des Mädchens Klage,' one of the most popular of his Lieder, but also of the less well known 'Hektors Abschied,' an alternating duet in operatic style, and

'Amalia' ('Schön wie Engel' from *Die Räuber*), which opens in a songlike manner but becomes declamatory. Although the 'social songs' received their best treatment in his male chorus settings, Schubert set a few as Lieder; his strophic 'An die Freude' is the best of all the 'functional' settings of this poem, but 'Die vier Weltalter' is very conventional. Among the best settings of the lyric poems are the sectional 'Der Alpenjäger;' 'Der Pilgrim,' sectional, hymnlike, and syllabic; the strophic and simple 'Der Jüngling am Bache' and 'Das Mädchen aus der Fremde;' and 'Die Hoffnung,' a splendid contrast to the simple version included in one of Reichardt's collections but, according to Friedlaender, not by this composer.[18] The hymn-like 'Thekla' consists of regular four-measure phrases but is distinguished by the magical alternation of major and minor characteristic of much of Schubert's music. A comparison of his early and later versions of the solo setting of 'An den Frühling,' one of the composer's favorite texts, shows his growth in musical maturity.

'Gruppe aus dem Tartarus,' one of the philosophical poems, is unquestionably the finest art-song to a text by Schiller. The principle of chromatic ascent, first melodically under a pedal point, then harmonically through the rest of the song, unifies the composition. Variety is provided not as much by the declamatory voice part as by the accompaniment. The climax is the exclamation of 'Ewigkeit!' in C major with strange shifts to the dominant of F♯ minor. The piano coda reverses the chromatic ascent by means of a descending C minor scale over a tonic pedal point. In this song the 20-year-old Schubert best solved the problem of setting music to the philosophical poem with classical allusions.

Schubert's most felicitous answers to the difficulties inherent in setting Schiller's complex prosody were to employ vocal declamation, characteristic of most of his songs to this poet's texts, or to use unconventional phrase patterns. 'An Emma,' one of Schiller's more difficult poems, is a good illustration: the song opens with a period composed of three six-measure phrases, then another period consisting of 4 + 4; 2 + 2, followed by a short recitative section and a declamatory passage containing fermatas, and concludes with a phrase pattern of 2 + 2 + 3. Less successful settings of the philosophical poems are 'Elysium,' sectional and with a wandering tonality, and 'Die Götter Griechenlands,' of which only the twelfth stanza is set; Schubert eulogizes Nature, not the Greek gods, and his vocal line is too florid for the elegiac character of the poem.

Among Schubert's least successful works are his settings of Schiller's ballades, most of which are early works and clearly show Zumsteeg's influence in their patchy and sectional construction and wandering tonalities. Some of these ballades are extremely long, especially 'Die Bürgschaft' and 'Der Taucher' with its 60-measure piano interlude. Einstein has described the two settings of 'Ritter Toggenburg' as being merely copies of Zumsteeg's version.[19] The sectional treatment is most successful in 'Die Erwartung,' but this approach fails in the better-known 'Sehnsucht,' described as 'made up of what looks like the material for a pianoforte sonatina;'[20] its mixture of styles, including military band effects and an incongruous operatic finale, is disturbing to the hearer. Best of all the ballades is the unjustly neglected 'Der Kampf,' a declamatory setting for bass voice underlaid by a persistent dotted figure in the accompaniment; the song is tonally unified, consistent, concise, and an excellent vehicle for the basso with a flair for dramatic declamation.

Nearly all of Schubert's song-settings of Schiller's texts are contained in the last four, rather than the more popular first three volumes of Friedlaender's edition of Schubert's songs, and later composers had only a fleeting interest in Schiller's poems as subjects for Lieder – one need only cite Spohr, Mendelssohn, Schumann, Liszt, Franz, Brahms, Grieg, Mac-Dowell, and Richard Strauss; the few exceptions, such as Liszt's and Taneiev's settings of the opening song of *Wilhelm Tell* or Brahms' 'Der Abend', only confirm the fact that Schiller's poetry was a negligible factor in the development of the Lied after 1820. Capell perhaps overstates the reason:

> [Schubert was] put off by something in Schiller that was prosaic and frigid...Schiller seems, on the strength of the songbooks, to miss the lyric note. His subjects are abstractions; there is no seizing and fixing a particular moment's vividness...Schubert gives the impression that Schiller was not a true lyric poet.[21]

A more likely reason was the greater suitability for Lieder of the lyric poems by such of Schiller's successors as Rückert, Hölderlin, Heine, and Mörike. Composers with an interest in setting Schiller's poetry turned to the choral medium.

2. *Choral Works*

Reichardt and Körner both saw that a long poem like 'Der Tanz' demanded greater musical resources than the Lied would permit. Reichardt told Schiller that his poem could be set only 'on a large scale and in full score,' whereas Körner even designated specific instruments at certain places, such as trumpets, clarinets, and basset horns at 'Es ist des Wohllauts.'[22] Many of Reichardt's settings of Schiller's 'social songs' are written for a soloist with choral refrain, and his best music to a poem by Schiller is his strophic choral setting of 'Die Ideale.'

Andreas Romberg was the first significant composer to write large-scale settings of Schiller's poems. Intermediate between the Lied with piano accompaniment and the cantata are his versions for soprano and orchestra of *Die Kindesmörderin, Der Graf von Habsburg*, and *Sehnsucht*, which in outline resemble the ballades for voice and piano by Zumsteeg or the young Schubert. Romberg's ballades do not contain set-numbers, and the composer frequently conceals the 'seams' by beginning a new section with a modulatory passage from the key of the preceding section to the new tonality. His settings exhibit more tonal unity and consistency than Zumsteeg's, but the music is hopelessly dated.

Of his large-scale settings, *Das Lied von der Glocke*

(1808) enjoyed immense popularity in England and the United States during the past century and is still performed in Germany, largely because of the straightforward and unpretentious nature of the composition and the simplicity of the solo and especially the choral parts; probably no other choral work is so easy to sing. Schiller himself had given instructions concerning the setting of this poem: when Körner told him of a version in Dresden which was a conglomeration of declamation, instrumental music, a few choral pieces, and music by various composers fitted to his text, the poet remarked: 'I thank God that I have not had to listen to that music (of which I have heard one of the movements here) and that performance' and specified that

> ...the 'Glocke' is very well suited to a musical representation, but then one must also know what is wanted and never scribble heedlessly... The Master Bellfounder holds the piece together. The music should never paint words and give itself to little trifles, but must only follow the spirit of the poetry as a whole.[23]

Romberg followed Schiller's instructions in that the Master Bellfounder (bass solo) gives the work the character of a rondo, frequently repeating to different words the melody of his opening song and thus unifying what would be an otherwise kaleidoscopic work. *Die Macht des Gesanges*, with its text repetition, recognizable set-numbers, and soprano solos which are more instrumentally than vocally conceived, was less successful; the work is imposing in a static sort of way but sounds too much like inferior Beethoven or Cherubini.*

Virtually all of the large-scale settings of Schiller's poems written during the nineteenth century have sunk into oblivion. Mendelssohn's *Festgesang an die Künstler* (based on 'Die Künstler'), for male chorus, solo male quartet, and brass, is a good example of the *Männerchor* literature of the 1840s. Its texture is basically homophonic except for the slightly contrapuntal middle section, and its sectional construction corresponds to the stanzas which the composer selected from Schiller's poem. The work does not deserve Eric Werner's strictures as being 'insignificant and bombastic' and having 'remained in manuscript – and rightly so,'[24] for the work was published as 'Ye Sons of Art' by G. Schirmer in 1907 and, despite its being out of print, is in the repertoire of the Men's Glee Club of Florida State University (Dr. Ramon Meyer, conductor) and is regarded as a very effective work. In contrast, Liszt's setting of this same poem (second version, 1856) for tenor solo, double male chorus, and orchestra approaches a climax of repetitiousness (one male chorus frequently answers the other with the same words). Max Bruch's *Das Lied von der Glocke* (1879) has the di-

---

* Romberg established the form of the choral ballade as unstaged dramatic cantata. It is therefore inaccurate to credit Mendelssohn's setting of Goethe's *Die erste Walpurgisnacht*, which in its structure owes much to Romberg's works, with being a new sort of cantata written without previous models.

mensions of an oratorio but is an omnium-gatherum of clichés and misfiring dramatic effects, whereas his *Dithyrambe* (ca. 1871) for tenor solo, six-part chorus, and full orchestra, although a better work, is unmistakably a 'period piece'.

The most significant large choral works based on Schiller's poetry are the choral finale of Beethoven's ninth symphony, based on several verses of 'An die Freude,' and Vincent d'Indy's curious *Le Chant de la cloche*. Beethoven originally intended to use, in the baritone recitative which opens the vocal portion of this movement, the words, set to a simple folk-like melody, 'Let us sing the song of the immortal Schiller,' but the text in the final version, as Sanders has recently conjectured, derives from Herder's conception of *das Angenehme*. The form of this movement is an immense theme and free variations in which elements of sonata-allegro structure, especially tonal relationships, are incorporated; it is not, as Sanders states, a modified sonata-allegro movement.[25] Such a formal organization in a choral work is perhaps unique.

Schiller's 'Das Lied von der Glocke' was merely a point of departure for d'Indy, who wrote the text as well as the music for *Le Chant de la cloche* between 1879 and 1883. The work is a life of Wilhelm, the Master Bell Founder, presented in a prologue and seven scenes: baptism, love, the festival, the vision, the fire, death, and triumph. Only in the fire scene does d'Indy adhere to Schiller's text; the stronger influence is Wagner's *Die Meistersinger*, for much hinges on the decision whether Wilhelm will be chosen Master Bell Founder; the four Beckmesser types (Pyk, Bitterli, Dumm, and Hartkopf) complain that his bell breaks the rules, is against tradition, and is incomprehensible; and the procession after the choral ballet in the festival scene owes much to the procession in Act III of Wagner's opera. Even stronger influences are d'Indy's ideas of artistic integrity and his fervent Catholicism, especially in the baptismal scene and Wilhelm's funeral during which the priests intone the 'In Paradisum' in the style of plainchant. The form of *Le Chant de la cloche*, like his later *La Légende de Saint Christophe*, lies between oratorio and opera; there is too much dramatic action for the former, whereas the problems of *mise en scène* in a manner approaching plausibility would be a nightmare for the stage director. Both these works demand more vocal and instrumental resources than the average conductor is willing to request in order to perform a major work by an excellent but currently unfashionable composer.

The shorter choral settings of Schiller's poems are at their best in Schubert's delightful compositions for an unjustly neglected and derided medium, the male chorus. The most enjoyable are 'An den Frühling,' with its 'La-la' refrain, the fragments from 'Der Triumph der Liebe,' and two of the three fragments from 'Elysium.' The accompanied short choral settings by Schubert consist of a rousing 'Punschlied' ('Vier Elemente') for male chorus and piano and the short, strophic 'Hymne an den Unendlichen' for mixed chorus with an independent piano part. Among the later exceptions to the trend during the nineteenth century toward clothing Schiller's longer poems in elaborate musical and instrumental garb, two exceptions are noteworthy: the once-popular *Männerwürde* ('Des Menschen Würde') for male chorus by Mendelssohn and Brahms' exquisite *Nänie*, Op. 82 (1881), for chorus and orchestra. It is no accident that the two most successful settings of Schiller's philosophical poems – Schubert's 'Gruppe aus dem Tartarus' and Brahms' *Nänie* – are musically consistent and concise settings of equally consistent and concise poems.

Parts of Schiller's poems served as texts for canons, a contrapuntal form which composers frequently wrote in the albums of their friends who could appreciate their polyphonic ingenuity. The 16-year-old Schubert made canonic settings of a fragment from 'Elysium' and, as a more interesting specimen, 'Sprüche des Konfuzius.' Spohr described the canon which he received from Beethoven as follows:

> ...a three-part canon to the words from Schiller's *Jungfrau von Orleans*, 'Kurz ist der Schmerz, und ewig währt [*recte* ist] die Freude!' It is worth noting that (1) Beethoven, whose handwriting of notes as well as of words was nearly unreadable, must have written this page with unusual patience, for it is unblotted from beginning to end, and what is even more remarkable, he drew the staff lines himself in freehand without a guide, and (2) right after the entrance of the third voice a measure is missing, which I have had to supply. The page is concluded with the wish 'May you, dear Spohr,

wherever you find true art and true artists, think
with pleasure of me, your friend.[26]

Although contemporary composers have virtually
ignored Schiller's poems as possible choral texts, a
few examples by German composers may be found.
Hugo Distler's *Das Lied von der Glocke* (1935), by one
of the few twentieth-century composers with a
thorough understanding of the problems of choral
composition, is a musically conservative and pan-
diatonic work with a formal link to Romberg's
setting in that the ten 'Meistersprüche,' (for tenor
soloist with choral response) consist of the same
music to different words, thus unifying the work
through the principle of rondo form. Distler uses
great restraint in scoring and, following Schiller's
instructions, avoids attempts at vivid tone-painting;
the most obvious sections, the fire and the burial, are
scored for solo voice and two pianos. He employs
a Baroque ideal of word-painting, capturing the
mood rather than trying to portray 'purple passages'
literally, and also uses Baroque terminology for the
episodal sections. He solves prosodic problems
through metric change within a phrase or, in climactic moments, speech rather than song. Occasionally a weak syllable comes on a musically strong
beat. Among the most effective sections are the
'Grabgesang' (Solo-Szene iv), spoken and later sung
by the soloist over a steady ostinato pattern, and the
use of the 'Marseillaise' (with rhythm and harmony
slightly altered), sung in French as background for
the declaimed 'Freiheit und Gleichheit!'

The choral settings of three of Schiller's poems by Carl Orff are of greater interest. *Nänie und Dithyrambe* (1956), scored for six flutes, four pianos (eight players), two harps, and several percussionists, but possible to perform with piano four hands and percussion orchestra, is similar in style to the opening chorus of his *Catulli Carmina*. A continuous pedal point sustained through both works is the chief unifying element. The constant metric changes in *Nänie* permit a free declamation (Orff's setting would be an excellent contrast to that of Brahms!), whereas *Dithyrambe* is mostly strophic with nonsense syllables in the coda. *Die Sänger der Vorwelt* (1956) is not as good a composition, for the repetition of the word 'kaum' has an unvocal sound and Orff uses fauxbourdon so frequently that it becomes a mannerism. Whereas Schubert emphasized Schiller's love of nature in 'Die Götter Griechenlands,' and d'Indy made the poet into a mediaeval Catholic, Orff in these settings transforms Schiller into a lusty pagan by bringing out the Dionysiac elements in his Grecian poems.

3. *Operas*

Although a few forgotten operas – Reichardt's *Der Taucher* and Schubert's and Kurt Weill's different settings of *Die Bürgschaft* – were based on Schiller's poems, all of his dramas, even the incomplete *Demetrius*, were converted into operas, and his adaptation of Gozzi's *Turandot*, translated into Italian by Count Maffei, gave Puccini the idea for his *Turandot*.[27] Several writers have commented on the similarity of Schiller's verse dramas to opera, and it is necessary only to cite Bruford's remarks that the atmosphere of these dramas approaches opera because they are 'works of a highly conscious type of art...deliberately anti-naturalistic in style, concerned with heroic themes and attempting to interpret the common fate of mankind.'[28]

Keys (and to a lesser extent Weigand) have discussed in detail most of the Italian operas based on Schiller's dramas, yet some supplementary remarks should be added to their studies. Rossini's *Guillaume Tell* (1829) contained enough of Schiller's original libertarian ideas to cause the opera to be censored in Italy and the portions of Eastern Europe under Tsarist domination. For instance, in Riga it had to be given as *Karl der Kühne* almost to the end of the nineteenth century.[29] Giuseppe Bardani's libretto to Donizetti's *Maria Stuarda* (1834) is 'poesia scritta sulla inspirazione della tragedia di Schiller.' Leicester and Mortimer are telescoped into one character, and throughout its career the opera was unsuccessful despite occasional attempts at revival, the last taking place in New York on 17 November 1964.

Saverio Mercadante's *I Brigante* (1836), omitted from Keys' study, is a condensation into three acts of *Die Räuber*. Among the many departures from Schiller's original play are the confidant Theresa, gratuitously awarded to Amalia so that she can explain the background of the drama for the audience, the meeting of Karl and Franz at the end of the first act, and Amalia's two *preghiere*, in keeping with the Romantic tendency to portray religious scenes on the stage. The second act is similar to the fifth scene of the fourth act of Schiller's play except that a monk, who also sings a *preghiera*, is old Moor's keeper. The third act includes Franz' dream, the storming of the castle, and Karl's leavetaking. The social ideals of the original are muted and the stage settings are picturesque in the pejorative sense of the term. Of the musical numbers I have been able to see only the two baritone arias, but they clearly show Mercadante as a transitional composer, for the accompaniment and recitatives often display the fire and drive of Verdi's early works, whereas the arias proper are replete with coloratura passages for the baritone in the style of Bellini or early Donizetti.

Verdi, the operatic composer most influenced by Schiller, based four of his operas on the poet's dramas. *Giovanna d'Arco* (1845), though derived from Schiller's most operatically conceived play, contains only four scenes which resemble incidents from the original: (1) the coronation march; (2) the 'recognition scene' between Giovanna and her father (named Giacomo, not Thibaut), (3) the watchtower scene in which Giacomo rather than a nameless soldier describes the progress of the battle, and (4) Giovanna's death, to which the librettist and composer add a funeral march; an ensemble in which Giovanna participates from her bier; a triple chorus of warriors, demons, and angels; and a high C for the heroine to sing in the measure before she expires. Her downfall comes not through her humility and doubt, as in Schiller's original drama, but through her love for Charles VII and her betrayal to the English by her father.

I Masnadieri (1847) is one of Verdi's most patronized compositions, chiefly because of a general lack of sympathy with its musical conventions and 'the lusty, uninhibited vulgarity of the younger Verdi.'[30] Count Maffei, Verdi's most literarily capable librettist next to Boito and the translator of many of Schiller's dramas into Italian, adapted *Die Räuber* for the operatic stage more skillfully than Crescentini did *I Brigante*. Although the libretto does not retain the songs of Amalia and Carlo (Karl), a delightfully bouncy and vulgar 'Coro di Masnadieri' in Act III takes the place of the 'Räuberlied.'

In *Luisa Miller* (1849), the best of Verdi's early Schiller settings, Wurm is a more important character than in the original drama (*Kabale und Liebe*) and Miller, with his coarseness removed, is changed into an old soldier, probably because of the Romantic tendency to consider musicians as inspired geniuses rather than sturdy lower-class characters. Weigand considers Cammarrano's libretto to be 'surprisingly good' in comparison to the general run of operatic librettos of the time,[31] and from a musical standpoint the opera ranks with *Nabucco* and *Ernani* as the best of Verdi's early works, though one is tempted to smile at such musical naivetés as Luisa's opening aria.

Méry and du Locle, the French adapters of *Don Carlo* (1867), ignored Schiller's statement that *Don Carlos* was the best work which he had created 'without the aid of spectacle and operatic décor,'[32] for the divertissements are for the sake of spectacle, the love interest of Carlo and Elisabetta is emphasized, the character of Princess Eboli is built up for vocal rather than dramatic reasons, and most of the subsidiary male personages are condensed into the Grand Inquisitor. Yet Posa's and Carlo's libertarian sentiments are openly displayed, and the climax of their duet is a virtual 'freedom leitmotiv' running throughout the opera. The last act, with the apparition of Charles v, is a tacked-on 'happy ending' which does not follow Schiller. The music, like that of Verdi's other operas between *La Traviata* and *Aïda*, belongs to a period of experimentation, of changing and deepening his musical style. The operas of this period tend to be long, contain many interesting harmonic and instrumental effects which were affected by the better moments in Meyerbeer's grand operas, and are better appreciated by singers and musicians than the general public.*

Schiller's dramas, which were well known in French and Italian translations, influenced the development of the librettos for the grand operas of the nineteenth century, principally in the broader dimensions in the portrayal of the villain and the concept of the 'flawed hero.' In the older 'rescue opera' the villain is a virtual incarnation of pathological monomania, like Pizarro in *Fidelio*; but although in Schiller's early dramas villains like Franz Moor,

* It is interesting to note that Verdi's Schiller operas were not at all popular in Germany during the nineteenth century, nor were any other operatic settings of this poet's dramas with the exception of Rossini's *Guillaume Tell*.

Spiegelberg, and Wurm fall into this category, the reader will find much more depth, plausibility, and even sympathy in the depictions of Philip II, Wallenstein, Elizabeth, and Thibaut, who are ancestors of the villain of high principle in Scribe's operas like Pietro in *La Muette de Portici*, Ankarström in *Gustave III* (Renato in Verdi's setting of the libretto as *Un Ballo in Maschera*), and Saint-Bris in *Les Huguenots*. Representative of the 'flawed hero' are Karl Moor, Fiesko, Don Carlos, and Mortimer; a strong parallel can be drawn between Fiesko and Masaniello, the first grand opera hero, and the ineffectual Mortimer of *Maria Stuart* can be found in many librettos, with Alfonso in *La Muette de Portici* and Nevers in *Les Huguenots* as good illustrations.

Although the trend was reversed during the middle of the nineteenth century, Schiller's dramas also helped to purge the opera of exotic elements. The libertarian ideas common to his dramas, the rescue operas, and the revolutionary operas were common to the time and not mutual influences; there is no evidence, for example, that Schiller ever heard the *Guillaume Tell* (1791) by Sédaine with music by Grétry. Ideas aside, Schiller's chief influence was upon characterization: after he wrote librettists more often created rounder and more complex characters than they had before.

Schiller as well as Sir Walter Scott contributed to the 'historicism' of the grand opera. Scott's historical novels were an even richer source of operatic librettos than Schiller's dramas, as witness such diverse works as Boieldieu's *La Dame blanche*, Carafa's *La Prison d'Edimbourg*, Marschner's *Templar und Jüdin*, and Bellini's *I Puritani*. And yet, although the pageantry, spectacle, and poetic licence of the historical grand opera may seem to be derived from Scott, these elements are present in their most obvious form in the much earlier *Die Jungfrau von Orleans* (1801), and the later gratuitous additions by librettists to Schiller's dramas were operatic conventions for which Schiller himself was at least partly responsible. Etienne Jouÿ, the librettist for *Guillaume Tell*, had also written the libretto for Gasparo Spontini's *La Vestale* (1807), the immediate ancestor of the historical grand opera.

Unlike the Italian operas based on Schiller's dramas, the later operas founded on his plays by non-Italian composers and librettists have been virtually unexamined and are at present almost completely unknown.

Schiller's drama *Fiesko*, despite its unheroic ending, would have been an ideal subject for the early Verdi because of its dramatic explosiveness, fine character delineation, and opportunity for the scintillating dance music and passionate vocal melodies at which he excelled. Bienefeld (and less convincingly, Schmidt-Garre) state that Verdi saw a performance of this drama in Cologne in 1877 and that it inspired a revision, performed in 1881, of his earlier *Simone Boccanegra* (1857)[33].

Eduard Lalo's *Fièsque* (1867), written in the same year as Verdi's *Don Carlo*, is the only operatic setting of this drama. Evidently it was never performed, although a vocal score was published. Hassan, the

Moor, is made an important character and even a kind of Arab Figaro. The best part of the opera is the third act with its male chorus of conspirators, the dramatic scene where the hero denounces Julia's attempt to poison the heroine, and a typically French terzetto in a seductive 9/8 meter. *Fièsque* merits a revival. I have been unable to see a score of Victorin de Joncières' *Dimitri* (1876), based on Schiller's unfinished *Demetrius*.

Fibich's *Nevěsta Messinská* (1884), popular in its day and even enjoying an occasional revival, is a work of high professional integrity and craftsmanship equal to that of any serious Czech opera. Although some of the choral writing follows Czech declamation in its use of 'Lombard rhythm,' the composer did not try to utilize 'folk' elements as Smetana and Dvořák did in their operas. Noteworthy here are the funeral march at the end and the antiphonal effect (as specified by Schiller) of the choirs, in which a four- and a five-part (including altos) male chorus sing in opposition; the choruses tend to overshadow the soloists in dramatic and musical importance. In outline Hustinský's libretto is quite faithful to the original drama.

Tchaikovsky wrote his own libretto, based on Zhukovsky's translation and adaptation of *Die Jungfrau von Orleans*, for his opera *Orleanskaya Dieva* (1881), a throwback to the grand operas of Halévy and Meyerbeer. Such divertissements as the choruses in Act I and the ballet music in Act II add to the opportunities for spectacle and pageantry already present in Schiller's drama, and the composer retained such characters as Dunois and Agnès Sorel. The 'confrontation scene' between Johanna, Thibaut, and the populace is more dramatically effective than in Verdi's setting. Johanna feels not compassion but love for Lionel, and the finale of the opera is somewhat more related to historical fact than is Schiller's ending: Lionel and Johanna are surprised by the English at the end of their love duet, Lionel is killed while defending her, and after a funeral march Johanna is burned at the stake. Her aria in Act I, 'Prostite vui, kholmui,' the only vocal portion of the opera to achieve any popularity, parallels her farewell to her humble village in the prologue of Schiller's drama, but her monologue in Act IV is absent from the opera. The orchestra plays an important role, not only in the scintillating ballet music but also in the entr'acte to Act II, a 'battle symphony' which foreshadows the first movement of his fourth symphony. The heroine must be portrayed by a powerful dramatic soprano who can sing over an often vigorous and noisy orchestra.

Only two twentieth-century operas of any significance have at this writing (1965) been based on Schiller's dramas: Jaromir Weinberger's *Valdštjn* (1937) and Giselher Klebe's *Die Räuber* (1956, revised 1962). *Valdštjn*, an excellent condensation of the *Wallenstein* trilogy into six scenes, retains the musical opportunities from the original dramas but the songs are given different texts: the 'Reiterlied' is set to the tune of the 'Pappenheimer March,' which recurs at the end of the fourth scene where Max leaves Thekla (comparable to *Wallensteins Tod*, III, 21); the 'Re-

krutenlied,' in the style of a Czech folksong, is sung
by the market-woman's niece; the banquet music and
Thekla's abortive aria are retained; and the equivalent
of 'Der Eichwald brauset' is a charming Tamburin
(the most delightful portion of the opera) which the
heroine later sings in the final scene when she learns
of Max' death. Weinberger strove to obtain accurate
declamation in the 'Kapuzinerpredigt' by putting the
Czech text and German translation on separate lines,
and Kareš' libretto is the best of any of the operatic
adaptations of Schiller's dramas. The music, though
very conservative by today's standards, is quite
effective; the opera should be performed.

Giselher Klebe's *Die Räuber*, for which he also
wrote the libretto, is the most novel of any of the
operas based on Schiller's dramas. Except for the
revised 'Räuberlied' he omitted the songs the dramatist specified, probably because they interrupt the
dramatic action which Klebe strove to maintain
without subsidiary interludes. The arias, of which
the most effective is Franz' dream in Act IV (V, 1), are
settings of the soliloquies, and the problem of
condensing a long drama is creatively solved in the
'double scene' of Act III in which the stage is divided,
with one half showing the Böhmerwald (II, 3 in the
original) and the other the garden in old Moor's
castle (III, 1); a quartet is then formed, with Karl and
the priest (an alto!) in the forest, Franz and Amalia
in the garden. Schoenberg and Berg are Klebe's
most obvious mentors, for the harmonic texture is
very dissonant, the vocal lines abound in difficult
intervals, and the accompaniment does not merely

support the voices but is an independent tonal web. Schmidt-Garre has pointed out some of Klebe's musical means of intensifying the opposition between the 'nihilist Franz' and the 'idealist Karl;' Franz is depicted by a tone-row with narrow intervals and is accompanied by 'the cold sound of a richly ornamented harpsichord part,' whereas Karl is portrayed by a tone-row with wide intervals and is accompanied by the 'solid, heavy sound of wind instruments.'[34]

4. *Program Music*

Whereas in vocal settings of Schiller's poems and dramas the listener has a text to follow, in program music, the final category of compositions based on the poet's works, the listener has only an abstract frame of reference for his guidance. The composer must assume that the performers and listeners are familiar with the subject he has selected and must choose, in works of any extent, either to decide on certain high points for literal or symbolic depiction or to attempt to capture the general mood of the literary work.

Die Jungfrau von Orleans inspired not only operas but also two rather curious pieces of program music. The 'Jungfrau von Orleans' piano sonata, Op. 46 (ca. 1868) by the English composer William Sterndale Bennett has not only captions (*e.g.*, 'Am Felde' or 'Im Gefängniss') but even passages of text for each movement; thus the finale bears the legend 'Kurz ist der Schmerz, und ewig ist die Freude!'

Bennett depicted the mood of the individual movement rather than specific incidents. The sonata itself
is of greater historical than musical interest, for it is
derivative and dull.

The symphonic poem *Johanna d'Arc*, Op. 19 (1879),
'nach Schiller's *Jungfrau von Orleans*' by Moritz
Moszkowski, a composer remembered today only
through his salon music, is one of the longest (316
pages of full score) of the works in this genre, but is
a representative example of the German symphonic
poem between Liszt and Richard Strauss. The first
movement depicts Johanna's shepherd life and her
vision, with the pastoral section harmonically,
melodically, and orchestrally too lush to portray
the simple shepherd girl accurately, and the movement is too long and repetitious to be convincing.
The second movement, 'Innere Zerwürfnisse –
Rückerinnerung,' an andante melancolico in 12/16
meter, tends to sag because of its rhythmic repetition.
The coronation march, a sort of 'Marche pontificale,'
contains a trio suspiciously reminiscent of Liszt's
Les Préludes and an especially noisy coda; it is too
slow, intricate, and long to be effective. The final
movement, depicting Johanna in prison, portrays
not only her release from her chains but also her
'Sieg, Tod, und Verklärung.' This movement, in
title and in several musical details, is a harbinger of
Richard Strauss' symphonic poem *Tod und Verklärung*, for Moszkowski's opening has some intervallic
similarity with Strauss' 'death struggle' theme, and
Moszkowski's march, battle music, and 'Risoluto'
(Kettensprung?) parallel similar passages in Strauss'
work. The heroine's death is announced by a

return of the angelic vision from the opening movement and her transfiguration by a noisy apotheosis
similar to those which conclude many of Liszt's
symphonic poems.

Although Schumann's overture to *Die Braut von
Messina*, Op. 100 (1851), may have been used for
dramatic performances, it is more in the character of
a program overture like those by Beethoven or
Mendelssohn than a prelude to the drama. A slow
introduction precedes a rapid passage in C minor in
the melodramatic style which derived from the 'Sturm
und Drang' and the battle symphony; this section is
followed by a lyrical clarinet solo, perhaps intended
to represent Beatrice. The coda is merely the first
theme played in a faster tempo, and the overture is
one of Schumann's least successful compositions.
An overture to this drama is included among Wagner's juvenilia.

That philosophical ideas are the most difficult to
express in music is clearly shown in Liszt's *Die
Ideale* (1857). The composer placed portions of
Schiller's poem, sometimes as many as 20 lines,
before individual musical sections as a guide to the
conductor, although the passages of text do not
necessarily indicate the formal divisions of the work.
An 'Apotheose' bears Liszt's footnote:

Adhering to, and thereby irresistibly manifest-
ing the Ideal, is the highest goal of our life. In
this sense I have allowed myself the enlarging of
Schiller's poem through the joyously affirmed re-

capitulation of the preceding motive of the first
section as a concluding apotheosis.

The apotheosis, and for that matter the entire
symphonic poem, is merely bombastic posturing.
The formal sense and thematic transformation which
Liszt used in an earlier and more musically grateful
philosophical composition, *Les Préludes*, are lacking
in what I think one of Liszt's least effective compositions.

The most successful symphonic poem based on
one of Schiller's works is Smetana's rousing and
exciting *Valdštýnův Tábor* (*Wallenstein's Camp*, 1859).
The brawling bustle of the opening gives place to a
march and some delightful folklike dance music
which is later used to interrupt the Capuchin's
sermon, stated in the trombones. The contemplative
andante and the trumpet fanfare, one of the most
thrilling in the literature, may be replaced by a
modulatory passage featuring a drum cadence if
this work is performed as an overture to the drama.
A martial tune, equivalent to Schiller's 'Reiterlied,'
ends the work.

Vincent d'Indy's symphonic trilogy *Wallenstein*,
Op. 12 (1873-81), consists of three individual symphonic poems, the best of which is *Le Camp de
Wallenstein* which lacks the directness and impact of
Smetana's composition but is still quite exciting;
in this poem d'Indy emphasizes not the 'Reiterlied'
but the waltz played by the miners. *Max et Thécla*,
the equivalent of *Die Piccolomini*, is based on the
opposition of sections of lyrical andante (Thekla)

with allegro risoluto (Max). *La Mort de Wallenstein* opens melodramatically but ends quietly. D'Indy does not depict specific incidents from his dramatic models, but rather captures the mood of what he feels to be the central theme of each drama.

Josef Rheinberger's *Wallenstein* (1866), Op. 10, is a large-scale 'symphonic tone-painting' in which strictly musical considerations take precedence over faithfulness to Schiller's trilogy. The opening 'Vorspiel' is a well-constructed but not very interesting sonata-allegro movement with no relationship to Schiller's plays; the second movement, 'Thekla,' sounds almost French because of its lyricism and compound meter; and the scherzo, 'Wallensteins Lager,' seems stodgy and heavy-footed when compared with Smetana's and d'Indy's compositions. The Dutch national anthem 'Wilhelmus van Nassau' is quoted as a 'Reiterlied from the era of the Reformation,' and the trio of the scherzo, a 'Kapuziner-Predigt,' was also published separately. The sectional final movement, 'Wallensteins Tod,' is inconsistent because the tragic mood of the opening is overdone, the middle section is almost gay, and the mood of the lyrical portion (adagio, 9/8, B major, which may represent the parting of Max and Thekla) is destroyed by the return of the middle section. The melodramatic coda ends like the opening 'Vorspiel,' but in minor.

A study of the music based on Schiller's works is like the 'core samplings' of geologists and oceanographers, for we have seen in this chapter important works by composers of stature side by side with minor works by major composers, inferior compositions, and meritorious works which are neglected because of changes in musical tastes. Only Schubert among the major composers fully did justice to Schiller's poems as Lieder, virtually all the nineteenth-century operatic settings must bear Weigand's verdict that the adaptations tended to bring out the 'latent melodramatic elements' without the 'restraining effect of his philosophy and poetic language,'[35] only Smetana's and d'Indy's symphonic poems would be welcome additions to the orchestral repertoire, and chiefly the choral works based on the poet's texts have fully done justice to his poetry. Generally, Schiller's countrymen did not succeed in setting his works as well as did composers of other nationalities. The reasons for the apparent lack of musical success of Schiller's works are not only the poet's elevated diction and dramatic and poetic length, or even the inadequacy of many of the composers who attempted to express ideas beyond their competence, but the shift in taste which has made Schiller's writings and nineteenth century music so unfashionable today. Another change in taste could easily bring about the revival of such meritorious but 'dated' works as d'Indy's *Le Chant de la cloche* and *Wallenstein*, Lalo's *Fièsque*, Fibich's *Nevěsta Messinská*, and Weinberger's *Valdštjn*.

The literature directly pertaining to the topic 'Schiller and Music' is scattered and of unequal value. The most nearly complete bibliographical lists are in Jürgen Mainka's 'Schiller und die Musik' in *Wissenschaftliche Zeitschrift der Friedrich-Schiller Universität* (Jena) V (1955-56), Gesellschafts- und Sprachwissenschaftliche Reihe, Heft 1, pp. 217-19, and the bibliography of Wolfgang Stockmeier's article 'Schiller' in MGG, XI, cols. 1719-20, although the most recent item listed therein is dated 1960. Annual lists of writings about Schiller, arranged according to topic, are published in the *Jahrbuch der deutschen Schillergesellschaft*.

The most satisfactory study of Schiller's direct relationship to music is Hans Knudsen's doctoral dissertation *Schiller und die Musik* (Greifswald, 1908). Marga Parzeller's article 'Schiller und die Musik' in *Goethe*, XVIII (1956), 282-94 and Martin Cooper's 'Schiller and Music' in *Adam*, XXVII (1959), 19-22, contain valuable insights but no documentation. Günther Kraft's *Schiller und die Musik*, a rehash of previous writings on this topic, is principally a guide to the planning of Schiller programs in schools but contains a short anthology of Schiller's poems in musical settings. Adolph Kohut's *Friedrich Schiller in seinen Beziehungen zur Musik und zu Musikern* (Stuttgart, 1905) is a journalistic study of little value. Franz Brandstaeter's *Gymnasium* program, *Über Schillers Lyrik im Verhältnisse zu ihrer musikalischen Behandlung* (Danzig, 1863), is not as restricted to song-settings as its title would suggest, but is rather the pioneering study on Schiller's relationship to

music and has a fairly complete listing of musical
settings of Schiller's poems and dramas.

CHAPTER ONE: MUSIC IN SCHILLER'S LIFE

The most important primary sources for information
concerning music in Schiller's life are Andreas
Streicher's *Schillers Flucht von Stuttgart und Aufenthalt
in Mannheim* (Stuttgart, 1838) and Karoline von
Wolzogen's *Schillers Leben* (Stuttgart and Tübingen,
1830, 2 vols.), written by the poet's sister-in-law.
The most valuable recent biographies and studies
were H. B. Garland's *Schiller* (London, 1949) and
Storm and Stress (London, 1952), and Reinhard
Buchwald's *Schiller: Leben und Werk*, 4th. edition
(Wiesbaden, 1949). For specific factual topics, the
biographies by Scherrl, Litzmann, Cysarz, Ernst
Müller, Witte, and Storz were of the greatest
assistance.

An anthology of first-hand accounts of Schiller's
musical experiences can be drawn from SP; much of
the same information is found also in Julius Peterson's *Schillers Gespräche* (Leipzig, 1911). The
different editions of Schiller's letters are Jonas;
Eduard Castle's "Carl Künzels 'Schilleriana,'" in
Akademie der Wissenschaft zu Wien (Philosophisch-
historische Klasse), Sitzungsberichte, 3te Abhandlung CCXXIX (1955); Geiger's collection of the letters
exchanged by Schiller and Körner; the Schiller-
Goethe correspondence translated by Dora Schmitz
(which must be compared with the German origi-

nals), and Ludwig Urlichs' *Briefe an Schiller* (Stuttgart, 1877).

Hermann Abert's *Niccolò Jommelli als Opernkomponist* (Halle, 1908) and 'Die dramatische Musik' in Württemberg Geschichts- und Altertumsverein, *Karl Eugen, Herzog von Württemberg und seine Zeit* (Esslingen, 1905-09, 2 vols.), I, 557-60, Rudolf Krauss' 'Das Theater' in the latter work, I, 485-554, and the chapter on Karl Eugen in Alan Yorke-Long's *Music at Court* (London, 1954) are the major studies on musical life in Württemberg during Schiller's childhood and are more recent than the nationalistic but informative book by Josef Sittard, *Zur Geschichte der Musik am Württembergische Hofe* (Stuttgart, 1890-91, 2 vols). I have discussed the musical program at the Karlsschule in "Music at the 'Hohe Karlsschule,' 1770-1794," *Journal of Research in Music Education*, XII (1964), 123-33.

W. H. Bruford's *Culture and Society in Classical Weimar* (London, 1962) renders all other accounts of the intellectual life in the Weimar of Goethe and Schiller virtually superfluous. The standard work about the musical life there is Wilhelm Bode's monumental *Die Tonkunst in Goethes Leben* (Berlin, 1912, 2 vols.) with detailed information about opera in Bruno Satori-Neumann's *Die Frühzeit des weimaranischen Hoftheaters unter Goethes Leitung 1791-1798*, SGTG, XXXI (1922). The subsequent literature on Goethe and music is copious but does not contain the detail to be found in Bode's study, but the short books on *Goethe und die Musik* by Abert (Stuttgart, 1922), Friedrich Blume (Kassel, 1948), and H. J.

Moser (Leipzig, 1949) are valuable for their insights;
Moser's volume also contains a comprehensive
anthology of little-known settings of Goethe's poems.
Herder's musical activity is partially discussed in
Walter Wiora's 'Herders Ideen zur Geschichte der
Musik' in Erich Keyser (ed)., *Im Geiste Herders*
(Kitzingen am Main, 1953) and "Herders und Hein-
ses Beiträge zum Theme 'Was ist Musik?'" in *Die
Musikforschung*, XIII (1960), 385-95, Wolfgang Nufer's
*Herders Ideen zur Verbindung von Poesie, Musik, und
Tanz* (Berlin, 1929), and F. E. Kirby's 'Herder on
Opera' in JAMS, XV (1962), 316-29. A full-scale
study of Herder's contributions to music is needed.

German opera between Mozart and Weber is
most thoroughly discussed in K. M. Klob's old but
valuable *Die Oper von Gluck bis Wagner* (Ulm, 1911),
and the rescue opera is treated in my 'Notes on the
Rescue Opera,' MQ, XLV (1959), 49-66. Naumann's
operas are examined in Richard Engländer's study
J. G. Naumann als Opernkomponist (Diss. Berlin,
1916).

CHAPTER TWO: MUSIC IN SCHILLER'S DRA-
MATIC WORKS

Incidental music in English drama is extensively
discussed in Emmett L. Avery's monumental *The
London Stage, 1660-1800* (Carbondale, 1960-   ),
Allardyce Nicoll's *A History of English Drama* (Cambridge, Eng., 1952, 4 vols.), and Montague Sommers'
The Restoration Theatre. The spread of the English
musical practice to Germany is well treated in Anna

Baesecke's *Das Schauspiel der englischen Komödianten in Deutschland* (Halle, 1935) and S. Mauermann's *Die Bühnenweisungen in deutschen Dramen bis 1700* (Berlin, 1911). Unfortunately most writers on 18th-century German drama have neglected the importance of incidental music; the best of the few exceptions are Albert Köster in his *Schiller als Dramaturg* (Berlin, 1891) and Bayard Quincy Morgan in his 'Goethe's Dramatic Use of Music,' PMLA, LXXII (1957), 104-112.

The standard studies of German incidental music are Franz Mirow, *Zwischenaktsmusik und Bühnenmusik des deutschen Theaters in der klassischen Zeit*, SGTG, XXXVII (1927), Adolf Aber's *Die Musik im Schauspiel* (Leipzig, 1926), and Wolfgang Golther's 'Die Musik in Schauspielen unserer Klassiker,' *Die Musik*, XXIV (1906-07), 273-84. An important primary source is G. K. Tolev's 'Etwas über die Musik beym Schauspiel,' *Allgemeine musikalische Zeitung*, VII (1805), cols. 805-09. Excellent recent surveys are Helmut Wirth's article 'Bühnenmusik' in MGG, II, cols. 431-47; Evans' article 'Incidental Music' in *Grove;* and Otto Riemer's 'Musik und Schauspiel' in Fred Hamel and Martin Hürlingen, eds., *Das Atlantisbuch der Musik*, 5th. ed. (Zürich, 1946), pp. 765-72. Satori-Neumann and Mirow discuss in great detail the performance of incidental music in Weimar; some information about this topic in Mannheim is given in Kurt Sommerfeld's *Die Bühneneinrichtungen des Mannheimer Nationaltheaters unter Dalbergs Leitung*, SGTG, XXXVI (1927).

The melodrama in the generally spoken drama is ignored in the 'standard' work on the subject, Jan

Van der Veen's *Le Mélodrame mnsical de Rousseau au Romantisme* ('s-Gravenhage, 1955), a study which needs to be redone.

Konrad Burdach's 'Schillers Chordrama und die Geburt des tragischen Stils aus der Musik,' DR, CXLII (1910), 232-62, and CXLIII (1910), 91-112, and Robert T. Clark, Jr's "The Union of the Arts in 'Die Braut von Messina,'" PMLA, LII (1937) are not only studies of *Die Braut von Messina* but also contain many excellent insights into Schiller's relationship to music. Valuable from a literary rather than a musical standpoint is Walter Silz' 'Chorus and Choral Functions in Schiller' in John R. Frey, ed., *Schiller 1759-1959* (Urbana, 1959), pp. 147-70.

The article 'Schiller' in *Grove* gives the most nearly complete listing of Schiller's incidental music; such lists can be found in Aber's and Brandstaeter's studies. The best investigation of Bernhard Anselm Weber's importance is still Robert Eitner's article 'B. A. Weber' in the *Allgemeine deutsche Biographie*, XLI (1896). Günther Kraft's article 'Kranz' in MGG, VII is the best work on this shadowy figure; Bode's remarks on Destouches are superior to the conflicting studies by Schaal (MGG) and Loewenberg (*Grove*).

CHAPTER THREE: MUSIC AS A LITERARY EF-
FECT

The few studies dealing with musicians in literature, such as George Schoolfield's *The Figure of the Musician in German Literature* (Chapel Hill, 1956) are almost exclusively concerned with the writings of the 19th and 20th centuries. My "Musical Portraits in 'Sturm und Drang' Drama" in M & L, XLVI (1965), pp. 39-49, discusses these musicians from a sociological viewpoint as well as the accuracy of their characterization, and contains a survey of the pertinent critical literature.

Brandstaeter and Knudsen admire rather than discuss Schiller's musical metaphors.

The literature on musical speech in German poetry of the second half of the 18th century is copious but of unequal value, owing to the prevailingly subjective interpretation of this phenomenon. Among the recent studies, Silz upholds this idea in 'On Rereading Klopstock,' PMLA, LXVII (1952), 744-68, Erny gives an excellent survey of this question, with many illustrations from primary sources, in 'Lyrische Sprachmusikalität als ästhetisches Problem der Vorromantik,' *Jahrbuch der deutschen Schillergesellschaft*, II (1958), 114-44; whereas K. L. Schneider, in his *Klopstock und die Erneuerung der deutschen Dichtersprache im 18. Jahrhundert* (Heidelberg, 1960), avoids the question of 'musical speech' and explains Klopstock's poetic language in technical prosodic terms.

In his *Schiller and the Changing Past* (London, 1957), William F. Mainland has an interesting discussion of Schiller's use of the word 'musikalisch' as a starting point for an assessment of the poet's ideas on music (pp. 160-80), but tends to overestimate Schiller's understanding of musical terminology.

CHAPTER FOUR: SCHILLER'S MUSICAL PHI-
LOSOPHY

Of the many studies on German musical aesthetics
during the 18th century, I have found the most
valuable, for this chapter, to be Schering's 'Künstler,
Kenner, und Liebhaber der Musik im Zeitalter
Haydns und Goethes,' JMP, XXXVII (1931), 9-23;
Hugo Goldschmidt's old but useful *Die Musik-
ästhetik des 18. Jahrhunderts* (Zürich and Leipzig,
1915), and Wolfgang Seifert's *Christian Gottfried
Körner* (Regensburg, 1960), which contains a fine
survey of German musical thought. The separate
literature which has grown up around Herder's and
Goethe's ideas on music is cited in the bibliographical essay for Chapter 1.

The general studies of Sulzer's *Allgemeine Theorie*
do not inform the reader that Sulzer did not write
the musical articles, although J. F. Reichardt announced this in his article 'J. A. P. Schulz' in *Allgemeine musikalische Zeitung*, III (1800), cols. 597-600.
His and Kirnberger's contributions are also assessed
in Carl Freiherr von Ledebur, *Tonkünstler-Lexikon
Berlins*, article 'Schulz' (Berlin, 1861), and Otto
Riess, 'Johann Abraham Peter Schulz' Leben,' *Sam-
melbände der internationalen Musikgesellschaft*, XV (1914-
15), 191 *et passim*. Kurt von Dadelsen in his article
'Kirnberger' (MGG, VII, col. 955) discusses Sulzer's
activity as Kirnberger's editor.

Richard Hohenemser's 'Schiller als Musikästheti-
ker,' *Die Musik* XV (1904-05), 192-203, and the
sections on Schiller's musical aesthetics in the studies

by Knudsen, Seifert and Mainland, are the only major examinations of the poet's musical philosophy, since the general surveys of musical aesthetics either omit or slight Schiller's thought. Outstanding as negative illustrations are Julius Portnoy's *The Philosophers and Music* (New York, 1954) and Rudolf Benz' *Die Welt der Dichter und die Musik* (Düsseldorf, 1949).

Works dealing with opera in Weimar are discussed in the bibliographical essay to Chapter 1. In addition, W. H. Bruford's *Theatre, Drama, and Audience in Goethe's Germany* (London, 1950) can be added as a study of the musical theatre from a socio-cultural viewpoint.

Bruford's *Weimar*, Reinhard Buchwald's *Schiller und Beethoven* (Waibstadt-Heidelberg, 1946), Burdach, *op. cit.*, and Marie Graves' *Schiller and Wagner* (Diss., Michigan, 1938) discuss Schiller's legacy to cultural thought in the 19th century.

CHAPTER FIVE: MUSICAL SETTINGS OF SCHIL-
LER'S WORKS

The standard studies of this topic are Brandstaeter, *op. cit.*, and Max Friedlaender's 'Kompositionen zu Schillers Werken,' DR, CXXIII (1905), 261-71, as well as his lists of 18th-century writers whose poems were set to music by their contemporaries in his *Das deutsche Lied im 18. Jahrhundert* (Stuttgart and Berlin, 1902, 3 vols.). These studies emphasize the Lieder written to Schiller's poems. Of the histories of 19th-century music Alfred Einstein's *Music in the*

Romantic Era (New York, 1947) contains the most information about Schiller's influence on subsequent composers. The literary parallels drawn by Helmut Schmidt-Garre in his *Oper: Eine Kulturgeschichte* (Cologne, 1963) are unconvincing, but in his *Schiller und Beethoven* Buchwald draws fine spiritual parallels between the two.

Ludwig Landshoff, in his *Johann Rudolf Zumsteeg* (Berlin, 1902), explores this composer's relationship to Schiller, and the quarrel between Schiller and Reichardt is intensively (though its musical basis is slighted) discussed in Geneviève Bianquis' 'En marge de la querelle des Xénies: Schiller et Reichardt,' *Etudes germaniques*, XIV (1959), 325-32, the basic source for most of the information about this quarrel in Walter Salmen's *Johann Friedrich Reichardt* (Freiburg i/B and Zürich, 1963). Alfred Einstein's *Schubert: A Musical Portrait* (New York, 1951) and (despite its anti-Schiller bias) Richard Capell's *Schubert's Songs* (New York and London, 1957) contain more information on Schiller and Schubert than do German studies of this composer. I have been unable to find a copy of Guido Adler's *Schiller und Schubert*, a lecture published in Vienna in 1910.

A. C. Keys' 'Schiller and Italian Opera,' M & L, XLI (1960), 223-37, and to a substantially lesser extent Paul Weigand's 'Schiller's Dramas as Opera Texts,' *Monatshefte*, XLVI (1954), 249-59, are the chief discussions of Italian operas based on Schiller's librettos. Because of its New York première on 17 November 1964, Donizetti's *Maria Stuarda* was discussed and reviewed in the local press (*New York*

Times, 15 and 18 November 1964, *New Yorker,* 28 November 1964).

In his *Schiller und die Musik* Günther Kraft gives on pp. 22-31 a list and brief anthology of Schiller settings suitable for commemorative programs. A sequel, 'Ballade und Einzellieder,' was announced 'in preparation' but has as yet not appeared.

NOTES

CHAPTER ONE

1 Andreas Streicher (ed. Hans Hofmann), *Schillers Flucht von Stuttgart und Aufenthalt in Mannheim* (Berlin, 1905), p. 4; SP, I, pp. 16, 29.

2 Percy Scholes (ed.), *Dr. Burney's Musical Tours in Europe* (London, 1959), 2 vols., II, 38.

3 SP, I, 33; Streicher, *op. cit.*, p. 15.

4 Streicher, *op. cit.*, p. 18.

5 Schiller to Körner, 30 April 1789.

6 SP, I, 38, 39; Johann Scherrl, *Schiller und seine Zeit* (Leipzig, 1859), p. 153.

7 Marga Parzeller, 'Schiller und die Musik, '*Goethe*, XVIII (1956), p. 285.

8 Streicher, *op. cit.*, p. 50.

8a SP, II, 2-3; 302-03.

9 Streicher, *op. cit.*, pp. 89-90.

10 *Ibid.*, pp. 100-01.

11 Schiller to Streicher, 8 December 1782.

12 Schiller to Henriette von Wolzogen, 26 May 1784; SP, II, 106.

13 Schiller to Körner, 10 February 1785.

14 Schiller to Huber, 13 November 1785.

15 *Leipziger Tageblatt*, 9 November 1859, cited in SP, II, 120; SP, II, 128, 84.

16 Schiller to Körner, 28 February 1802.

17 Reinhard Buchwald, *Schiller: Leben und Werk*, 4th. ed. (Stuttgart, 1959), p. 721.

18 Schiller to Körner, 23-24 July 1787; Jonas VII, cv; Schiller to Körner, 28-31 July 1787.

19 Schiller to Körner, 12 August 1787; Jonas, I, 392.

20 Schiller to Körner, 6 October 1787.

21 Schiller to Körner, 28 July 1787.

22 B. Litzmann, *Schiller in Jena* (Jena, 1889), p. 41.

23 Schiller to Körner, 8 December 1787.

24 Schiller to Körner, 1 November 1790.

25 SP, II, 182-83.

26 Schiller to Körner, 23 February, 18 November 1795; 17 March 1802.

[27] Julius Peterson, *Schillers Gespräche* (Leipzig, 1911), p. 340; Amy Fay, *Music Study in Germany*, 18th. ed. (New York, 1909), p. 153.

[28] Karoline von Wolzogen, *Schillers Leben* (Stuttgart and Tübingen, 1830, 2 vols.), II, 70-71, 296.

[29] Charlotte Schiller to Karoline von Humboldt, 27 October 1822.

[30] Alfred Meissner, *Rococo-Bilder* (1876), cited in SP, II, 204; Schiller-Körner correspondence, 11 January-1 May 1797; Geiger, III, 402.

[31] Peterson, *loc. cit.*

[32] SP, III, 142.

[33] Wolzogen, *op. cit.*, II, 270.

[34] Voss to Griesbach, 13 May 1805.

[35] Schiller to Huber, 17 May 1786.

[36] Körner to Schiller, 20 April 1787.

[37] Schiller to Körner, 19 December 1787; Körner to Schiller, 24 December 1787.

[38] Gerhard Storz, *Der Dichter Friedrich Schiller* (Stuttgart, 1959), pp. 463-64.

[39] SA, VIII, 310-11.

[40] Zumsteeg to Schiller, 12 February 1800.

[41] Körner to Schiller, 7 October 1801; Schiller to Körner, 18 October 1801; Körner to Schiller, 25 October 1801.

[42] Peterson, *op. cit.*, pp. 364-65; Weber to Schiller, 20 March 1804.

[43] Schiller to Goethe, 11 May 1798.

[44] Schiller to Iffland, 14 April 1804.

[45] C. W. Oemler, *Schiller oder Szenen und Characterzüge aus seinem späteren Leben* (Stendal, 1805), p. 41; SP, I, 99; Ludwig Urlichs, *Charlotte von Schiller und ihre Freunde* I, 113, cited in Hans Knudsen, *Schiller und die Musik* (Diss. Greifswald, 1908), pp. 7-8.

[46] SP, I, 166; II, 224-25, 251, 297; III, 29.

[47] Voss to Börn, 2 May 1804.

CHAPTER TWO

[1] 'The Green Room,' cited in Emmett L. Avery, *The London Stage, 1660-1800* (Carbondale, 1960-), I, cxxxvi.

[2] Johann Adolf Scheibe, *Der Critische Musicus*, 67. *Stück* (8 December 1739), pp. 319-26.

[3] Johann Christoph Gottsched, *Versuch einer critischen Dichtkunst*, 3d. ed. (Leipzig, 1742), p. 723.

[4] Scholes, *op. cit.*, II, 75.

[5] Friedrich Schröter and Richard Theile, eds., *Lessings Hamburgische Dramaturgie* (Halle, 1877), pp. 159-72.

[6] J. G. Robertson, *Lessing's Dramatic Theory* (Cambridge, England, 1939), p. 486.

[7] Thomas Evans, 'Incidental Music' in *Grove*, IV, 451.

[8] SA, XVI, 295.

[9] 'Über das gegenwärtige teutsche Theater,' SA, XI, 82.

[10] Schiller to Grossmann, 5 April 1787; 'Über Egmont, Trauerspiel von Goethe,' SA, XVI, 190.

[11] G. K. Tolev, 'Etwas über die Musik beym Schauspiel,' *Allgemeine musikalische Zeitung* VII (1805), cols. 805-09.

[12] Schiller to Iffland, 26 April 1800.

[13] Bayard Quincy Morgan, 'Goethe's Dramatic Use of Music,' PMLA, LXXII (1957), 104.

[14] Knudsen, *op. cit.*, p. 44.

[15] Wolfgang Golther, 'Die Musik in Schauspielen unserer Klassiker,' *Die Musik*, XXIV (1906-07), 280.

[16] Herbert Stubenrausch, *Die Räuber* (Weimar, 1953), pp. 319-20.

[17] Schiller to Schröter, 18 December 1786; Parzeller, *op. cit.*, p. 288.

[18] Schiller to Goethe, 31 December 1798.

[19] Bruno Satori-Neumann, *Die Frühzeit des weimaranischen Hoftheaters unter Goethes Leitung 1791-1798*, SGTG, XXXI (1922), 122-24.

[20] Walter Silz, 'Chorus and Choral Functions in Schiller,' in John R. Frey, ed., *Schiller 1759-1959* (Urbana, 1959), p. 167.

[21] Golther, *op. cit.*, p. 293.

[22] Konrad Burdach, 'Schillers Chordrama und die Geburt des tragischen Stils aus der Musik,' DR, CXLIII (1910), 93; Robert T. Clark, jr., 'The Union of the Arts in *Die Braut von Messina*,' PMLA, LII (1937), 1142.

[23] 'Über den Gebrauch des Chors in der Tragödie,' SA, XVI, 123, 125-26.

[24] Schiller to Zelter, 28 February 1803.

[25] Schiller to Iffland, 24 February 1803.

[26] Buchwald, *op. cit.*, p. 773.

[27] Franz Mirow, *Zwischenaktsmusik und Bühnenmusik des deutschen Theaters in der klassischen Zeit*, SGTG, XXXVII (1927), 59.

[28] Schiller to Dalberg, 8 September 1781; SA, XVI, 19.

[29] Mirow, *op. cit.*, p. 57.

[30] Schiller to Zelter, 6 July, 7 August 1797; Zelter to Schiller, 14 July 1797; Schiller to Körner, 20 October 1797.

[31] Zumsteeg to Schiller, 24 September 1797; Schiller to Cotta, 15 December 1797, 5 January 1798.

[32] Schiller to Goethe, 20 January 1802, 3 August 1804.

[33] Schiller to Zelter, 16 January 1804; Schiller to Iffland, 20 February 1804.

[34] SP, III, 239.

[35] Quoted in Mirow, *op. cit.*, p. 101.

[36] Garlieb Merkel's review of *Wilhelm Tell* in *Der Freimüthige, oder Ernst und Scherz*, 7 July 1804.

[37] Hans Heinrich Borcherdt, *Schillers Werke: Bühnenbearbeitungen* (Weimar, 1949), I, 306.

CHAPTER III

[1] Knudsen, *op. cit.*, pp. 41-42.

[2] Günther Kraft, *Historische Studien zu Schillers Schauspiel 'Die Räuber'* (Weimar, 1959), pp. 7, 50, 121, 123.

[3] *Kurtzgefasstes musikalisches Lexikon* (Chemnitz, 1737), pp. 201, 356; Hermann Fischer, *Schwäbisches Wörterbuch* (Tübingen, 1914), art. 'Kunstpfeifer;' H. C. Koch, *Musikalisches Lexikon* (Frankfurt a/M, 1802), art. 'Stadtmusikus;' H. J. Moser, *Musiklexikon*, 5th. ed. (Hamburg, 1955), art. 'Zunftwesen.'

[4] J. W. Schottländer (ed.), *Carl Friedrich Zelters Darstellungen seines Lebens*, Schriften der Goethe-Gesellschaft, XLIV (1931), 40.

[5] Goethe to Schiller, 13 January 1804.

[6] Arthur Loesser, *Men, Women, and Pianos* (New York, 1954), pp. 60-63, 66.

[7] *Königliche priviligierte Berlinische Staats- und gelehrte-Zeitung*, 6 September 1784.

[8] Sulzer, II, 659; J. G. Herder, 'Kritische Wälder' in Suphan, IV, 94.

[9] Friedrich Schiller, 'Über das gegenwärtige teutsche Theater,' SA, XI, 84.

[10] Hans Lutz, *Schillers Anschauungen von Kultur und Natur* (Berlin, 1928), pp. 46, 53.

[11] Herder, 'Kritische Wälder,' Suphan IV, 48.

[12] Edward A. Lippman, 'Hellenic Conceptions of Harmony,' JAMS, XVI (1953), 3-5.

[13] Knudsen, *op. cit.*, p. 79.

[14] Burdach, *op. cit.*, CXLII (1910), 239; Gerhard Fricke, *Studien und Interpretationen* (Frankfurt a/M, 1956), p. 52; Wilhelm Dilthey, *Von deutscher Dichtung und Musik* (Leipzig, 1933), pp. 307-08, 302.

[15] John Brown, *A Dissertation on the Rise, Union, and Power, the Progressions, Separations, and Corruptions of Poetry and Music* (London, 1763), pp. 27-28, 196-98; J. G. Hamann, 'Aesthetica in Nuce' in Josef Nadler (ed.), *Johann Georg Hamann: Sämtliche Werke* (Vienna, 1950), II, 197; J. G. Herder, 'Abhandlung über den Ursprung der Sprache' in Suphan, V, 57 and 'Versuch einer Geschichte der lyrischen Dichtkunst' in Suphan, XXXII, 107.

[16] G. E. Lessing, *Laokoon* in *Gesammelte Werke*, V (Berlin, 1958), 112; Sulzer, II, 368.

[17] Knudsen, *op. cit.*, p. 32.

[18] Herder, 'Kritische Wälder,' Suphan, IV, 110-11.

[19] Friedrich Schiller, 'Über naive und sentimentalische Dichtung,' SA, XII, 209.

[20] Friedrich Schiller, 'Über Matthissons Gedichte,' SA, XVI, 260; Schiller to Körner, 25 May 1792; Schiller to Goethe, 18 March 1796.

[21] Zelter to Schiller, 20 February 1798.

[22] Walter Silz, 'Antithesis in Schiller's Poetry,' *Germanic Review*, XXXIV (1959), 171; Schiller to Körner, 25 September 1801; Gerhard Storz, *Der Dichter Friedrich Schiller* (Stuttgart, 1959), p. 340.

[23] Bayard Quincy Morgan, 'Musical Pitch in Goethe's Poetry,' *Monatshefte*, LV (1963), pp. 98-100.

CHAPTER FOUR

[1] Sulzer, III, 5 and II, 5-7; Hermann Kretzschmar, 'I. Kants Musik-auffassung und ihr Einfluss auf die folgende Zeit,' JMP, XI (1904), 43-56; Arnold Schering, 'Künstler, Kenner, und Liebhaber der Musik im Zeitalter Haydns und Goethes,' JMP, XXXVIII (1931), 12.

[2] 'Philosophie der Physiologie,' SA, XI, 34; 'Zusammenhang der tierischen Natur des Menschen mit seiner Geistigen,' SA, XI, 67.

[3] SA, XI, 57, 40.

[4] Schiller to Körner, 25 February 1789; 11 January, 5 May, 20 June 1793; Körner to Schiller, 18 January, 11 May 1793; Knudsen, *op. cit.*, pp. 24-25.

[5] Max Friedlaender, *Das deutsche Lied im 18. Jahrhundert* (Stuttgart and Berlin, 1902, 3 vols.), I, xxxviii; his 'Kompositionen zu Schillers Werken,' DR, CXXIII (1905), 266; Knudsen, *op. cit.*, p. 23.

[6] Körner to Schiller, 28 March 1794.

[7] Knudsen, *op. cit.*, p. 24; Wagner, *op. cit.*, I, 234; Schiller to Reinwald, 9 December 1782.

[8] 'Briefe über die ästhetische Erziehung des Menschen,' SA, XII, 83-85. (R. Snell's translation, New Haven, 1954, pp. 104-05.)

[9] Ästhetische Erziehung,' SA, XII, 55; Snell, *op. cit.*, pp. 76, 120.

[10] 'Über Matthissons Gedichte,' SA, XVI, 259.

[11] 'Über die notwendigen Grenzen beim Gebrauch schöner Formen,' SA, XII, 138.

[12] Schiller to Körner, 23 February 1793.

[13] Schiller to Körner, 3 February 1794.

[14] Abert, *Goethe*, p. 59; Richard Hohenemser, 'Schiller als Musik-ästhetiker,' *Die Musik*, XV (1904-05), 192-93; Irving Babbitt, 'Schiller as Aesthetic Theorist' in *On Being Creative and Other Essays* (Boston and New York, 1932), pp. 150, 179.

[15] Bruford, *Weimar*, p. 279.

[16] Edward J. Dent, *Mozart's Operas* (London, 1913), p. 14.

[17] Carl Philipp Emanuel Bach (tr. William Mitchell), *Essay on the True Art of Playing Keyboard Instruments* (New York, 1949), p. 152; Sulzer (K-S), III, 424.

[18] Knudsen, *op. cit.*, p. 17; 'Über Matthissons Gedichte,' SA, XVI, 258-59.

[19] 'Das gegenwärtige teutsche Theater,' SA, XI, 87.

[20] Sulzer, II, 55 and (K-S) III, 574; see also note 10.

[21] Snell, *op. cit.*, pp. 104-05; SA, XII, 83-85.

[22] 'Schema über den Dilettantismus,' SA, XII, 324-25.

[23] 'Zerstreute Betrachtungen über verschiedene ästhetische Gegen stände,' SA, XI, 275; 'Über Anmut und Würde,' SA, XI, 241; Snell, *op. cit.*, pp. 82-83.

[24] Immanuel Kant, *Kritik der Urteilskraft* (Leipzig, 1878), pp. 51-54; Sulzer, I, 144; J. G. Herder, *Kalligone* in Suphan XXII, 27-28, 30; 'Über das Pathetische,' SA, XI, 250-51.

[25] Brown, *op. cit.*, p. 198; Charles Avison, *Essay on Musical Expres sion*, 3d. ed. (London, 1775), p. 39; Benjamin Franklin to Peter Franklin in John Bigelow (ed.), *The Complete Works of Benjamin Franklin* (New York and London, 1887), III, 393.

[26] Sulzer (K-S), III, 438; Vernon Gotwals (ed. and trans.), *Joseph Haydn* (Madison, 1963), p. 125.

[27] Martin Cooper, 'Schiller and Music,' *Adam: International Review*, XXVII (1959), 21.

[28] 'Notwendige Grenzen,' SA, XII, 124-25.

[29] Hohenemser, *op. cit.*, p. 200.

[30] E.g., Sulzer (K-S), III, 431-32; Brown, *op. cit.*, pp. 36, 47; J. G. Herder, 'Von der Musik der Psalmen,' Suphan, XV, 249.

[31] Schiller to Körner, 18 August 1787. Hoffmann-Erbrecht (MGG, V, col. 1301) erroneously gives the date as 1788.

[32] Burdach, *op. cit.*, p. 21; 'Über Anmut und Würde,' SA, XI, 245.

[33] Walter Wiora, 'Herder,' MGG, VI, col. 203; Körner to Schiller, 4 October 1801; Hermann Hettner, *Geschichte der deutschen Litera tur im 18. Jahrhundert* (Leipzig, 1928, 3 vols.), III, 177; Bode, *op. cit.*, I, 275.

[34] Knudsen, op. cit., p. 64; Schiller to Goethe, 24 May 1803.

[35] Schiller to Körner, 5 January 1801.

[36] Körner to Schiller, 28 March 1794, 18 June 1797, 29 March 1802, 18 January 1801.

[37] Wolfgang Seifert, *Christian Gottfried Körner* (Regensburg, 1960), pp. 21-22.

[38] Schiller to Dalberg, 7 June 1784.

[39] Schiller to Körner, 10 February 1785 and 2 February 1789; Schiller to Grossmann, 5 April 1787.

[40] Buchwald, *Schiller*, pp. 107-08.

⁴¹ Walter Serauky and Hans Haase, 'Gottsched,' MGG, V, col. 576; Sulzer (K-S), III, 572-78; Edith Amelia Runge, *Primitivism and Related Topics in Sturm und Drang Literature* (Baltimore, 1946), pp. 240-41.

⁴² Schiller to Goethe, 18 March 1796 and 24 December 1800; Schiller to Körner, 5 January 1801.

⁴³ Schiller to Wilhelm von Wolzogen, December 1787.

⁴⁴ Schiller to Goethe, 29 December 1797.

⁴⁵ Schiller to Goethe, 28 April 1801, 17 December 1800, 19 January 1799, 2 and 5 May 1797, 12 May 1802; Schiller to Charlotte, 20 March 1801.

⁴⁶ Goethe to Schiller, 30 December 1797; Körner to Schiller, 28 March 1794; Seifert, *op. cit.*, pp. 24-25.

⁴⁷ Peterson, *op. cit.*, p. 365.

⁴⁸ Erich Hertzmann, 'Mozart's Creative Process,' MQ, XLIII (1957), 199.

⁴⁹ Suphan, XXIII, 335-38, 345.

⁵⁰ 'Über Anmut und Würde,' SA, XI, 245; SP III, 136-37.

CHAPTER FIVE

¹ Godfrey Ehrlich, 'Die gegenseitige Wiederannäherung von Dichtkunst und Musik im 18. Jahrhundert,' *Monatshefte*, XXVIII (1936), 299; Hermann Abert, 'Wort und Ton in der Musik des 18. Jahrhunderts,' *Archiv für Musikwissenschaft*, V (1923), 54-56.

² Körner to Schiller, 30 July 1797, 29 September 1795.

³ Körner to Schiller, 10 February 1802.

⁴ Friedlaender, 'Kompositionen,' p. 264.

⁵ SA, XVI, 19; Ludwig Landshoff, *Johann Rudolf Zumsteeg* (Berlin, 1902), p. 37.

⁶ Schiller to Cotta, 16 June and 21 July 1797; Schiller to Goethe, 23 July 1797, 11 February 1802; Schiller to Haug, 5 March 1802; Schiller to Körner, 17 March 1794.

⁷ Schiller to: Lotte von Lengefeld and Karoline von Beulwitz, 30 April 1789; to Körner, 30 April 1789; to Reichardt, 10 July 1795; to Cotta, 25 September 1795; Goethe to Schiller, 16 May 1795.

⁸ Schiller to Reichardt, 3 August 1795; Eduard Castle, "Carl

Künzels 'Schilleriana,'" *Akademie der Wissenschaft zu Wien* (Philosophisch-historische Klasse), Sitzungsberichte, 3te Abhandlung CCXXIX (1955), 60; Schiller to Körner, 31 August 1795; Körner to Schiller, 9 September 1795.

9 Goethe to Schiller, 31 January 1796; Schiller to Goethe, 5 February 1796; Körner to Schiller, 28 January 1796.

10 Schiller to Amalie von Imhoff, 4 October 1797; Schiller to Körner, 5 October 1801; Walter Salmen, *Johann Friedrich Reichardt* (Freiburg i/B and Zürich, 1963), pp. 89-90.

11 Salmen, *ibid.*, p. 90.

12 Schottländer, *op. cit.*, p. xvii; Goethe to Schiller, 25 June and 10 October 1796; Schiller to Goethe, 24 June 1796; Schiller to Zelter, 8 and 18 August 1796.

13 Zelter to Goethe, 25 November 1823, 13 November 1830, both cited in SP, III, 165-66.

14 Körner to Schiller, 20 June 1802.

15 Körner to Schiller, 2 May 1802; Friedlaender, *Das deutsche Lied*, I, xxxviii.

16 Zelter to Goethe, 13 November 1830, cited, in SP III, 165; Schiller to Körner, 2 and 23 September 1801; Seifert, *op. cit.*, p. 16.

17 Georg Knepler, *Musikgeschichte des XIX. Jahrhunderts* (Berlin, 1960-61, 2 vols.), II, 631-32.

18 Friedlaender, *Das deutsche Lied*, II, 397.

19 Alfred Einstein, *Schubert: A Musical Portrait* (New York, 1951), pp. 27, 122.

20 Richard Capell, *Schubert's Songs* (New York and London, 1957), p. 31.

21 *Ibid.*, p. 11.

22 Schiller to Körner, 31 August 1795; Körner to Schiller, 9 September 1795.

23 Körner to Schiller, 25 February 1805; Schiller to Körner, 5 March 1805 (his last letter concerning music).

24 Eric Werner, *Mendelssohn* (London, 1963), pp. 439, 417.

25 Ernest Sanders, 'Form and Content in the Finale of Beethoven's Ninth Symphony,' MQ, L (1964), 72-76.

26 Ludwig Spohr, *Selbstbiographie* (Cassel and Göttingen, 1860-61, 2 vols.), I, 213; facsimile facing p. 216.

27 Mosco Carner, *Puccini: A Critical Biography* (London, 1958), p. 210.

[28] *E.g.*, Parzeller, *op. cit.*; p. 286; Herbert Cysarz, *Schiller* (Halle, 1934), p. 363; H. B. Garland, *Schiller* (London, 1949), pp. 237, 220; Storz, *op. cit.*, p. 340; Bruford, *Weimar*, pp. 365-66.

[29] Alfred Loewenberg, *Annals of Opera* (2d. ed., Geneva, 1955), cols. 719-20.

[30] Donald J. Grout, *A Short History of Opera* (New York, 1947), pp. 316-17.

[31] Paul Weigand, 'Schiller's Dramas as Opera Texts,' *Monatshefte* XLVI (1954), 257.

[32] Schiller to Grossmann, 5 April 1787.

[33] Elsa Bienefeld, 'Verdi and Schiller,' MQ, XVII (1931), 206-07; Helmut Schmidt-Garre, *Oper: eine Kulturgeschichte* (Köln, 1963), pp. 270-72.

[34] Schmidt-Garre, *ibid.*, p. 398.

[35] Weigand, *op. cit.*, p. 259.

INDEX

II. INDEX OF PROPER NAMES

UNIVERSITY OF NORTH CAROLINA
STUDIES IN THE GERMANIC LANGUAGES
AND LITERATURES

PD
25
.N6   Longyear
No.54   Schiller and music

Date Due
